A Guide to Statistical Sources in Money, Banking, and Finance

The rare Arabian Oryx is believed to have inspired the myth of the unicorn. This desert antelope became virtually extinct in the early 1960s. At that time several groups of international conservationists arranged to have 9 animals sent to the Phoenix Zoo to be the nucleus of a captive breeding herd. Today the Oryx population is over 400, and herds have been returned to reserves in Israel, Jordan, and Oman.

Copyright © 1988 by The Oryx Press
2214 North Central at Encanto
Phoenix, Arizona 85004-1483

Published simultaneously in Canada

All rights reserved
No part of this publication may be reproduced or transmitted in any form or by any means, electronic or mechanical, including photocopying, recording, or by any information storage and retrieval system, without permission in writing from The Oryx Press.

Printed and Bound in the United States of America

∞ The paper used in this publication meets the minimum requirements of American National Standard for Information Science—Permanence of Paper for Printed Library Materials, ANSI Z39.48, 1984.

Library of Congress Cataloging-in-Publication Data

Balachandran, M.
  A guide to statistical sources in money, banking, and finance.

  Includes indexes.
    1. Finance—Statistics—Bibliography. 2. Money—
Statistics—Bibliography. 3. Banks and banking—
Statistics—Bibliography. 4. Finance—Statistics—
Data bases—Directories. I. Title.
Z7164.F5B23   1987   [HG171]   016.332′021   87-21941
 ISBN 0-89774-265-6

A Guide to Statistical Sources in Money, Banking, and Finance

by M. Balachandran

Phoenix • New York
ORYX PRESS
1988

Contents

Introduction vii
State Sources 1
Regional Sources 11
National Sources 18
Foreign Country Sources 43
International Sources 64
Databases 78
Directory of Publishers 87
Title Index 99
Subject Index 113

Introduction

This book is a selected and annotated bibliography of mainly serial reference sources dealing, more or less exclusively, with banking and monetary statistics. They relate not only to the United States but also to other countries and regions. This bibliography will help researchers identify and locate those publications that cover in detail specific information on capital and credit markets, interest rates, consumer finance and credit cards, money supply and currency, treasury operations, bank deposits, bank loans, assets, liabilities and profitability of financial institutions, and foreign exchange markets. It will also help reference librarians charged with developing and/or perfecting a core collection of materials in this area.

Banking and monetary data are normally available from numerous statistical compendiums dealing with national economic statistics. However, because of space limitations in them, these sources may not deal with this topic in as much detail or for as long a timespan as researchers in this area require. They must, therefore, resort to publications issued, for example, by central banks, which for the most part are responsible for the conduct of their countries' monetary policies. Also under this category are publications issued by state and local agencies that have regulatory jurisdiction over banking and financial institutions. International agencies like the International Monetary Fund and commercial publishers like Euromoney Publications collect and disseminate a wide array of statistical data relating to banking and monetary topics. This book attempts to identify and bring together such sources.

The contents of this volume have been grouped under the following categories: state sources, regional sources, national sources, foreign country sources, international sources, and databases. The directory of publishers lists the addresses of important government agencies and institutions, both U.S. and foreign, and also private firms, that publish banking and monetary statistics. The subject and title index at the end of the volume provides access to sources of information emanating from governmental institutions, international organizations, trade associations, private banks, and commercial publishers.

State Sources

ALABAMA

1. Alabama. Department of Banking. *Annual Report of Superintendent of Banks of the State of Alabama, for the Fiscal Year Ending September.* Montgomery, AL. Annual.

Report on financial condition of Alabama state-chartered financial institutions, presenting consolidated balance sheet data and/or income and expenses for commercial banks, small loan licensees, consumer credit agencies, and credit unions, with selected comparisons. Also includes assets of individual banks, savings and loans, and credit unions, arranged by city or rank; deposits of individual banks; small loan licensees and consumer credit agency operations, with detail for delinquent account legal actions; and credit union membership, loan operations, and earnings distribution. Contains lists of Department of Banking officials and of bank status changes. In addition to the annual report, information on new charters for banks is available from a monthly bulletin, *New Applications: Receipt and Actions Taken.*

ALASKA

2. Alaska. Department of Commerce and Economic Development. *Comparative Statement of Assets, Liabilities, and Capital Accounts of Alaska Banks.* Juneau, AK. Quarterly.

Report on the financial condition of Alaska state-chartered commercial and mutual savings banks as well as national banks, by institution and type. Contains among other things comparative statements of assets, liabilities, subordinated notes/debentures, equity capital, and comparative consolidated condition statements. More extensive statistics on the state's banking activities are available from the *Annual Report* of the Director of Banking, Securities and Corporations Division.

ARIZONA

3. Arizona. Banking Department. *Condensed Statement of Reports of State and Federal Savings and Loan Associations.* Phoenix, AZ. Quarterly.

Covers assets, liabilities, and equity capital of the savings and loans doing business in the state. Includes information on the number of branch offices. The Banking Department publishes a companion quarterly, *Condensed Statement of Reports of State and National Banks of Arizona,* which reports on assets, liabilities, equity capital, and the number of branch offices of the state and national banks. Information on actions taken on the approval of new charters is available from the monthly *Summary of Actions on Applications Received.* The financial condition of consumer finance companies licensed to operate in the state is analyzed in the *Annual Report of the Consumer Finance Companies.* Among other things, the report gives data on composite balance sheets, income statements, loan activities, and delinquent accounts. Also lists licensees by city and type of license.

ARKANSAS

4. Arkansas. Bank Department. *Report of the Bank Commissioner.* Little Rock, AR, 1913– . Annual.
Deals with the financial condition of state-chartered banks, trust companies, and industrial loan institutions. Compiled from the call reports filed with the Bank Department, this annual presents data on assets, liabilities, and equity capital of the above financial institutions and lists banking officials and facilities. Data are arranged by city and type of institution.

CALIFORNIA

5. California. Banking Department. *Annual Report of the Superintendent of Banks.* San Francisco, CA, 1909– . Annual.
Deals with the financial condition of all banks and trust companies doing business in the state. Presents assets, liabilities, income, and expenses for state and national banks, foreign banks with offices in California, and trust companies. Includes data on bank applications, openings and closings, mergers, and licensing and other regulatory activities. Also ranks top 25 banks by deposits. The Department also publishes a *Weekly Bulletin* containing updated information and news of activities.

COLORADO

6. Colorado. Department of Regulatory Agencies. *Annual Report of the State Bank Commissioner.* Denver, CO, 1909– . Annual.
Presents data on the financial condition of state-chartered commercial and industrial banks and trust companies in terms of assets, liabilities, and equity capital. Data are given both for the aggregate and for the institutions. Also includes loan activity, new bank charters, and capital changes. The Department also publishes an annual report, *Financial Report on Colorado State Charter Savings and Loan Associations,* covering assets, liabilities, net worth, composite financial and operating data, and a directory of savings and loan associations in the state.

CONNECTICUT

7. Connecticut. Department of Banking. *Annual Report of the Banking Commissioner.* Hartford, CT. Annual.
   Deals with the financial condition of state-chartered financial institutions. Presents data on assets, liabilities, income, and expenses by institution and other financial and operating data for state banks and trust companies, savings banks, savings and loans, credit unions, and small loan licensees. Includes information on bank holding companies, national banks, and federal savings and loans. Also provides a directory of most of the financial institutions covered in the report.

DELAWARE

8. Delaware. Department of Administrative Services. *Annual Report of the State Bank Commissioner.* Dover, DE, 1919– . Annual.
   Deals with the financial condition of state financial institutions, e.g., commercial banks, nondeposit trust companies, mutual savings banks, national savings banks, small loan companies, and state and federally chartered savings and loans. Data for institutions include assets, liabilities, capital, and deposit and loan activity.

FLORIDA

9. Florida. Office of the Comptroller. Division of Banking. *Annual Report.* Tallahassee, FL, 1895– . Annual.
   Deals with the financial condition of state-chartered financial institutions, national banks, and international bank agencies. Information presented on these institutions includes assets, liabilities, capital, operating income and expenses, bank operating ratios, ranking of banks by assets, and total bank employment. Financial data are also available for bank holding companies.

GEORGIA

10. Georgia. Department of Banking and Finance. *Annual Report.* Atlanta, GA, 1919– . Annual.
   Analyzes the financial condition of the state's financial institutions in terms of assets, liabilities, capital, income, expenses, loan activity, interest rates, and licensing. Institutions included are state and national banks, state-chartered credit unions, savings and loans, bank holding companies, and international bank agencies.

HAWAII

11. Hawaii. Division of Financial Institutions. *Comparative Statement of Condition.* Honolulu, HI. Annual.
   Covers state-chartered banks, savings and loans, trust companies, and industrial loan companies.

IDAHO

12. Idaho. Department of Finance. *Annual Report.* Boise, ID, 1919– . Annual.
> Presents data on assets, liabilities, equity capital, and net worth for state-chartered banks, savings and loans, and credit unions. Also includes composite balance sheet data for national banks and composite financial and loan activity of state-regulated lenders and credit unions. Information is given on bank consumer loans by purpose and delinquencies.

ILLINOIS

13. Illinois. Commissioner of Banks and Trust Companies. *Annual Report.* Springfield, IL. Annual.
> Deals with the financial condition of state-chartered banks and trust companies. Data cover assets, liabilities, capital/surplus, and profits/reserves for individual banks and trust companies, arranged by city; assets of licensed foreign banks, arranged by institution; resources and liabilities of institutions with trust powers; number of banks; and income and expenses. A companion annual report, *Resources and Liabilities of Illinois State Banks at the Close of Business*, contains similar information.

14. Illinois. Department of Financial Institutions. *Annual Report.* Springfield, IL. Annual.
> Analyzes the financial condition of state-chartered credit unions in terms of their assets, shares, membership, lending activity, mergers, liquidations, operating ratios, balance sheets, income, and expenses. Some of the data are arranged by type of credit union and by county.

15. Law Bulletin Publishing Co. *Chicago Banks.* Chicago, IL, 1958– . Semiannual.
> Provides detailed information on the financial condition of banks in Chicago.

INDIANA

16. Indiana. Department of Financial Institutions. *Annual Report.* Indianapolis, IN, 1935– . Annual.
> Deals with the financial condition of state-chartered financial institutions, such as banks, industrial loan and investment companies, building and loan associations, pawn brokers, and credit unions. Composite data include assets by type, liabilities, income, and expenses, all arranged by individual institution and location. Also includes data on balance sheet ratios.

IOWA

17. Iowa. Department of Banking. *Annual Report of the Superintendent of Banking.* Des Moines, IA, 1946– . Annual.
> Presents condition statements of financial institutions, including banks; trusts; and small loan, money order, and debt management companies.

For each institution, arranged by city, data on assets, liabilities, equity capital, composite income, expenses, financial ratios, loan activity, and delinquent accounts are provided. Also given are lists of state banking officials, banks, and loan licensees.

KANSAS

18. Kansas. Banking Department. *Comparative Abstract.* Topeka, KS. Annual.
Summarizes statements of condition for state banks and trust companies in terms of assets and liabilities. The monthly *Changes in Kansas State Banks for the Month of...* contains significant new developments.

KENTUCKY

19. Kentucky. Department of Banking and Securities. *Annual Report of the Commissioner.* Frankfort, KY, 1912– . Annual.
Analyzes the financial condition of state-chartered banks, trust companies, credit unions, savings and loans, industrial loan companies, and licensed consumer loan companies. Consists of five different annual reports covering various types of financial institutions. For most of these, individual as well as aggregate data, arranged by city, are provided, including trends regarding assets, expenditures, loan activity, and other statistics relating to performance ratios. Also includes directories of the financial institutions covered.

LOUISIANA

20. Louisiana. Department of Commerce. Financial Institutions Office. *Reports of the State Banks, Savings and Loan Associations, Credit Unions, Consumer Credit and Sale of Checks in the State.* Baton Rouge, LA. Annual.
Analyzes the condition of the financial institutions in the state in terms of assets, liabilities, net worth, number of banks, bank facility and capital stock increases, composite bank operating ratios, income, expenses, and loan activity. Most of the data are arranged by institution and by city. More current information on banks as well as savings and loans is available from the *Monthly Bulletin of Changes in Bank Activity.*

MAINE

21. Maine. Department of Business, Occupational and Professional Regulation. *Annual Statistical Report of the Bureau of Banking.* Augusta, ME. Annual
Presents aggregate financial data on financial institutions arranged by type of institution, county, and state economic areas. Includes assets, deposits, shares, loan activity, number of institutions, and other data relating to performance measures. Coverage includes commercial banks, trust companies, national banks, savings and industrial banks, credit unions, and state and federal savings and loans.

MARYLAND

22. Maryland. Department of Licensing and Regulation. *Annual Report of the Bank Commissioner.* Baltimore, MD, 1910– . Annual.

Analyzes the financial condition of state-chartered banks, trust companies, mutual savings institutions, credit unions, and secondary loan mortgage companies. Information includes assets, liabilities, equity capital, income, expenses, loan activity, and financial ratios, arranged by institution. Also lists financial institutions and licensees.

MICHIGAN

23. Michigan. Department of Commerce. Financial Institutions Bureau. *Annual Report.* Lansing, MI, 1888– . Annual.

Reports on the financial condition of the state-chartered commercial banks, savings and loans, safe/collateral deposit companies, credit unions, loan companies, and bank holding companies. Presents data on consolidated assets, liabilities, income, expenses, operating ratios, and loan activities.

MINNESOTA

24. Minnesota. Department of Commerce. Division of Financial Institutions. *Annual Report.* St. Paul, MN. Annual.

Provides consolidated statements of condition for state commercial banks, state banks, trust and investment companies, national banks, foreign banks, and credit unions.

MISSISSIPPI

25. Mississippi. Department of Banking and Consumer Finance. *Annual Report.* Jackson, MS. Annual.

Presents the statements of condition of Mississippi financial institutions, such as commercial banks, credit unions, and small loan companies. Includes a list of banks, branches, and other financial institutions by location. Provides data on assets, liabilities, equity capital, income, and expenses.

26. Mississippi Bankers Association. *Mississippi Bank Directory.* Jackson, MS. Annual.

Provides financial and related information on banks and their branches in the state. The annual is partially updated by the monthly *Mississippi Banker.*

MISSOURI

27. Missouri. Department of Economic Development. Commissioner of Finance. *Report.* Jefferson City, MO. Biennial.

This report, together with a quarterly *Abstract*, provides composite data on the banks in the state.

MONTANA

28. Montana. Commissioner of Financial Institutions. *Abstract of Condition*. Helena, MT. Annual.
Covers state banks and trust companies as well as national banks. Provides aggregate resources and liabilities as well as significant financial ratios.

NEBRASKA

29. Nebraska. Department of Banking and Finance. *Annual Report*. Lincoln, NE. Annual.
Presents composite financial data on state-chartered commercial banks, savings and loans, cooperative credit associations, credit unions, trust companies, industrial loan and investment companies, and installment loan companies. Includes information on bank capital, income, expenses, and earnings, all arranged by the size of the institution.

NEW HAMPSHIRE

30. New Hampshire. Banking Department. *Annual Report of the Bank Commissioner*. Concord, NH, 1844– . Annual.
Presents statements of condition of such financial institutions as commercial banks, trust companies, mutual/guaranty savings banks, cooperative banks, credit unions, retail sellers, finance companies, and small loan licensees. Data, arranged by city and institution, include assets, liabilities, income, expenses, and selected operating ratios.

NEW JERSEY

31. New Jersey. Department of Banking. *Annual Report of the Commissioner*. Trenton, NJ. Annual.
Presents assets and liabilities of the state-chartered commercial banks, savings banks, credit unions, insurance premium finance companies, pawnbrokers, secondary mortgage companies, small loan companies, savings and loans, and state cemetery board trust funds. Includes rankings of some types of institutions.

NEW MEXICO

32. New Mexico. Regulation and Licensing Department. Financial Institutions Division. *Annual Report*. Santa Fe, NM, 1913– . Annual.
Presents the statements of condition of state and federally chartered financial institutions, such as commercial banks, savings and loans, and credit unions. Data include assets, liabilities, equity capital, net worth, number of branches, income, expenses, loan activity, and selected financial ratios.

NEW YORK

33. New York. Superintendent of Banks. *Annual Report.* Albany, NY. Annual.
> Provides a statement of condition of the banking institutions in the state. Data include assets, liabilities, income and expenses, loan activity, and selected financial ratios.

NORTH CAROLINA

34. North Carolina. Commissioner on Banks. *Annual Report.* Raleigh, NC. Annual
> Provides balance sheet information on the state's financial institutions, including trust companies and bank holding companies. Consumer finance licensees are covered by a separate annual report.

NORTH DAKOTA

35. North Dakota. Department of Banking and Financial Institutions. *Report of the Commissioner.* Bismarck, ND. Biennial.
> Reports on the statements of condition for banks, trusts, credit unions, small loan and consumer finance companies, collection agencies, and money brokers.

OKLAHOMA

36. Oklahoma. Banking Department. *Report of the Bank Commissioner.* Oklahoma City, OK. Annual.
> Reports on the financial condition of state-chartered banks, trust companies, savings and loans, and credit unions. Presents financial and operating ratios by type of institution.

OREGON

37. Oregon. Department of Commerce. *Report of the Superintendent of Banks.* Salem, OR, 1907– . Annual.
> Presents the statements of condition of state banks and trust companies, credit unions, consumer finance companies, national banks, and pawnbrokers. In addition to information on assets, liabilities, revenues, expenses, and profits, the report gives data on the number of banks and deposits and loan activity, by institution and location. More current information is available from the quarterly *Abstract of Condition.*

PENNSYLVANIA

38. Pennsylvania. Department of Banking. *Annual Report.* Harrisburg, PA. Annual.
> Contains comparative consolidated reports of condition and listings of the state's savings institutions, credit unions, chartered banks, trust companies, bank holding companies, foreign banks, and secondary mortgage loan companies.

RHODE ISLAND

39. Rhode Island. Department of Business Regulation. *Annual Report of the Banking Division.* Providence, RI, 1907– . Annual.
   Gives composite balance sheet and income statement data on state-chartered commercial banks, trust companies, loan and investment companies, building and loan associations, credit unions, finance companies, national banks, and federal savings and loans. Data in most cases are arranged by institution.

SOUTH DAKOTA

40. South Dakota. Division of Banking and Finance. *Comparative Abstract.* Pierre, SD. Annual.
   Contains statements of condition for state banks. Includes data on assets and liabilities, revenues, expenses, profits, deposits, and loan activity.

TENNESSEE

41. Tennessee. Department of Financial Institutions. *Annual Report.* Nashville, TN. Annual.
   Deals with the financial condition of state-chartered banks, credit unions, savings and loans, and bank holding companies. Presents data on assets, liabilities, income, expenses, bank operating ratios, and loan activity.

TEXAS

42. Bankers Digest Inc. *Banker's Digest.* Dallas, TX, 1942– . Weekly.
   Contains news and commentary as well as financial data on individual banks in Texas.

43. Bankers Digest Inc. *Texas Banking Red Book.* Dallas, TX, 1947– . Annual.
   Provides financial and related information on all the banks in Texas. Also includes a list of executives.

UTAH

44. Utah. Department of Financial Institutions. *Report of the Commissioner.* Salt Lake City, UT. Annual.
   Deals with the financial condition of state-chartered banks, commercial banks and trust companies, savings/building and loan associations, national banks, industrial loan corporations, credit unions, and supervised lenders. Data arranged by institution include selected balance sheet and income statement items. A list of the institutions dealt with in the report is included.

VERMONT

45. Vermont. Department of Banking and Insurance. *Annual Report of the Bank Commissioner.* Montpelier, VT. Annual.

Analyzes the financial condition of state-chartered financial institutions, commercial banks and trust companies, mutual savings banks, savings and loans, credit unions, and licensed lenders. In addition to composite financial and operating data on these institutions, rankings of the different types of institutions by assets are also included.

VIRGINIA

46. Virginia. Corporation Commission. Bureau of Financial Institutions. *Annual Report.* Richmond, VA. Annual.

Provides individual as well as aggregate financial and operating data on state-chartered banks, mutual and stock savings and loans, industrial loan associations, credit unions, and other financial institutions.

WASHINGTON

47. Washington. Department of General Administration. Banking Division. *Annual Report of the Supervisor of Banking.* Olympia, WA, 1916– . Annual.

Presents the statements of condition for state-chartered commercial and savings banks, trust companies, industrial loan companies, consumer finance companies, and branches of foreign banks. Individual as well as aggregate data are provided for assets, liabilities, income, expenses, bank financial and operating ratios, and aggregate loan activity.

WISCONSIN

48. Wisconsin. Office of the Commissioner of Banking. *Annual Report.* Madison, WI, 1894– . Annual.

Contains a financial analysis of the banks in the state in terms of earnings, asset size, loan activity, and capitalization. In addition to reports of condition, there are selected financial ratios for the banks covered.

Regional Sources

49. The Chicago Corporation. *Midwest Bank Survey.* Chicago, IL, 1985– . Quarterly.

Handy reference guide which provides comprehensive information compiled from a survey of 350 Midwestern banks in Illinois, Indiana, Iowa, Kentucky, Michigan, Minnesota, Missouri, Ohio, and Wisconsin. Data include individual performance ratios, prices, earnings, book values, assets, loans, and primary capital. Other information covers completed and pending mergers, including price, asset size, type of consideration, price/book value, and closing date. Also includes bank rankings based on performance and price.

50. Federal Home Loan Bank Board. *Savings and Loan Institutions Deposits by Market in the Chicago SMSAs.* Washington, DC, 1985– . Annual.

Reports on the assets and deposits of the Seventh District's savings institutions, arranged by institution and market area. The district covers Illinois and Wisconsin. Includes a ranking of the associations by assets and some comparative statistics by counties.

51. Federal Home Loan Bank of Atlanta. *Annual Report.* Atlanta, GA. Annual.

Includes information on member banks, financial conditions and operations, and a directory of banks and bank officers. It reports on the operations of member institutions in Alabama, Florida, Georgia, Maryland, North Carolina, South Carolina, Virginia, and Washington, DC. The semiannual *Estimated Member Information* contains figures for ratio analysis in terms of assets, liabilities, loans, deposits, and investments. The bank also publishes *Quarterly Statistics,* which contains data on the number of reporting institutions, assets, mortgage loan activity, mortgage-backed securities issued, liabilities, net worth, savings, and lending activity by type. The triennial *Review of Federal Home Loan Bank of Atlanta, Fourth District,* contains statistics on savings and loans and their operations. Articles published deal with topics like worth ratio, profit variability, return on assets, and market competition.

52. Federal Home Loan Bank of Boston. *Annual Report.* Boston, MA. Annual.

Contains a directory of members as well as their financial statements reporting on their conditions and operations. Member banks are located in Connecticut, Massachusetts, Maine, New Hampshire, Rhode Island,

and Vermont. The bank's annual *Factbook* analyzes the financial conditions of savings institutions, commercial banks and cooperative banks. It provides information on mortgage and savings activity and selected balance sheet items for financial ratio analysis.

53. Federal Home Loan Bank of Chicago. *Annual Report.* Chicago, IL. Annual.

Contains detailed information on the financial conditions and operations of member banks in Illinois and Wisconsin. Two monthly publications from the bank, entitled *Home Mortgage Commitment Rates in Illinois* and *Home Mortgage Commitment Rates in Wisconsin,* survey monthly mortgage loan commitment interest rates for savings and loans in the two states. Tables show average effective and contract rates and fees on conventional adjustable rate mortgages and figures for loan/price ratio analysis. Another monthly, called *Index Report,* contains index numbers for the cost of funds, mortgage interest rates, savings and loan activity, and national comparisons for savings institutions in Illinois and Wisconsin. Data on the number of insured institutions, their offices, and the volume of savings broken down by county in both states are available from the annual *Insured Savings and Loan Institutions' Savings by County in Illinois and Wisconsin.* A monthly newsletter called *Seventh District Letter* deals with savings and loan industry operations in Illinois and Wisconsin. It covers savings flows, and mortgage loans closed by SMSA and county.

54. Federal Home Loan Bank of Cincinnati. *Annual Report.* Cincinnati, OH. Annual.

Contains detailed information on the financial conditions and operations of member banks in Ohio, Kentucky, and Tennessee. The quarterly *Economic Trends and Cycles* contains information on mortgage market activity in Kentucky, Ohio, and Tennessee in terms of mortgage interest rates, loan activity and commitments, assets, and liabilities of member institutions. Also contains national information on money supply and interest rates. The bank's monthly *Highlights* deals with the financial conditions and operations of savings and loans. Data include financial flows, number of savings and loans, assets, deposits by type, advances and borrowings, outstanding loan commitments, and figures for ratio analysis. Data are arranged by state and SMSA. Publication has been temporarily suspended. The bank's *Quarterly Review* is devoted to articles on the operations of savings and loans and housing finance. However, selected issues contain performance analysis of savings and loans in terms of profitability, interest rate risk exposure, cash management, and portfolio risk.

55. Federal Home Loan Bank of Dallas. *Annual Report.* Dallas, TX. Annual.

Analyzes the operations of member banks in Arkansas, Louisiana, Mississippi, New Mexico, and Texas. The monthly *District Data Highlights* deals with financial conditions and operations of insured savings institutions. It shows the number of reporting institutions, assets, loan activity, deposits, mortgages outstanding, net worth, and net income. Data are arranged by SMSA.

56. Federal Home Loan Bank of Des Moines. *Annual Report.* Des Moines, IA. Annual.

Contains detailed information on financial conditions and operations of member institutions in Iowa, Minnesota, Missouri, North Dakota, and South Dakota. Includes information on bank mergers. The bank's *Monthly Statistical Report* updates the information on the operations of savings and loans. It shows data on adjustable mortgage loan indexes; treasury bill yields; average interest rates of major lenders; average cost of funds; and figures for ratio analysis, including assets, outstanding mortgages, savings, deposits, net worth, and loan commitment type. This report was originally entitled *The Trends.* Similar data are also available in *Quarterly Statistical Report.*

57. Federal Home Loan Bank of Indianapolis. *Annual Report.* Indianapolis, IN. Annual.

Provides information on the financial condition and operations of member institutions in Indiana and Michigan. The bank's quarterly publication *Financial Information Report, Quarterly Report Aggregates* deals with financial conditions and operations of savings institutions in Indiana and Michigan. Aggregate data cover the number of reporting institutions, assets, liabilities, net worth, operating income and expenses, sources and uses of funds, and figures for financial ratio analysis. The data are updated in the monthly *Financial Information Report,* which shows contract and effective mortgage interest rates for home loans, selected interest balance sheet items, loan activities and commitments, and figures for financial ratio analysis.

58. Federal Home Loan Bank of New York. *Annual Report.* New York, NY. Annual.

Contains summary analysis of the financial conditions and operations of member banks in New York, New Jersey, Puerto Rico, and the Virgin Islands. Data include deposit and loan activity, assets, liabilities and net worth, and selected financial ratios.

59. Federal Home Loan Bank of Pittsburgh. *Annual Report.* Pittsburgh, PA. Annual.

Contains data on the financial conditions and operations of member banks in Delaware, Pennsylvania, and West Virginia.

60. Federal Home Loan Bank of San Francisco. *Annual Report.* San Francisco, CA. Annual.

Contains data on the financial conditions and operations of member banks in Arizona, California, and Nevada. Updated information on the same is available from the bank's *Quarterly Report.* The quarterly *Perspectives* deals with operations of savings institutions, including data on investments, outstanding mortgages, total assets, deposit by type, net worth, and loan activity. It continues in part a now discontinued publication, *Economic and Housing Indicators,* which contained similar data. The quarterly *Savings and Loan Summary Statistics* includes selected balance sheet items, loan commitments, cash and investments, outstanding mortgages, deposits, sources and uses of funds, and loan activity. Another quarterly, *Savings Balances and Accounts,* contains a directory of member institutions. It includes data on number of accounts and savings balances arranged by state, county, SMSA, and city.

61. Federal Home Loan Bank of Seattle. *Annual Report.* Seattle, WA. Annual.

Analyzes the financial activities of member banks in Alaska, Hawaii, Guam, Idaho, Montana, Oregon, Utah, Washington, and Wyoming. Its monthly *Twelfth District Highlights* provides updated information on the financial conditions of member institutions, including data on savings deposits, mortgage loan activity, general loan activity, and savings flows.

62. Federal Home Loan Bank of Topeka. *Annual Report.* Topeka, KS. Annual.

Deals with the financial conditions and operations of member institutions in Colorado, Kansas, Nebraska, and Oklahoma. The monthly *Economic Indicators* contains data on savings and loan activity by the members. *Monthly Financial Data* reports on the financial conditions and operations of member institutions. It includes information on assets, mortgages, loan activity, loan commitments, and savings deposits, arranged by state and SMSA.

63. Federal Reserve Bank of Atlanta. *Annual Report.* Atlanta, GA. Annual.

This Federal Reserve district includes Alabama, Florida, Georgia, and parts of Louisiana, Mississippi, and Tennessee. The report deals with the region's economic and financial developments and includes indicators of the area's economy, such as deposits at commercial banks, credit unions, and savings and loans; mortgage loan activity; and commitments. It also contains a statement of condition, earnings, and expenses of the Federal Reserve Bank of Atlanta. The monthly *Economic Review* updates most of the statistical information contained in the *Annual Report*.

64. Federal Reserve Bank of Boston. *New England Economic Indicators.* Boston, MA. Monthly.

First Federal Reserve District includes Maine, Vermont, New Hampshire, Massachussetts, Rhode Island, and Connecticut. Includes the following indicators: deposits held at savings institutions, weekly report of condition of commercial banks, consumer installment credit outstanding by type of credit, mortgage loan activity, and interest rates on regular mortgages at selected thrift institutions.

65. Federal Reserve Bank of Chicago. *Annual Report.* Chicago, IL. Annual.

The Seventh Federal Reserve District includes Iowa, Illinois, Indiana, Michigan, and Wisconsin. The *Annual Report* presents data on the loan activities and deposit transactions of the banks in the district. The bimonthly *Economic Perspectives* focuses on banking and financial developments. The monthly *Midwest Update* and biweekly *Agricultural Letter* also deal with the district's financial conditions.

66. Federal Reserve Bank of Cleveland. *Annual Report.* Cleveland, OH. Annual.

The Fourth Federal Reserve District includes Ohio, Kentucky, Pennsylvania, and West Virginia. The report contains statements on financial conditions and income. The quarterly *Economic Review* deals with economic and financial developments in the Fourth District. A companion monthly, *Economic Trends,* is a compilation of data on financial indicators such as money supply, monetary aggregates, velocity of money, bond and equity markets, borrowing and saving by sectors, and selected foreign exchange rates.

67. Federal Reserve Bank of Dallas. *Annual Report.* Dallas, TX. Annual.
The Eleventh Federal Reserve District includes Texas and parts of Louisiana and New Mexico. Its *Annual Report* presents a financial summary showing statements of condition, income, expenses, volume of operations, and bank holding company activity. The bimonthly *Economic Review* contains in-depth analysis of regional and international finance. The *Quarterly Survey of Agricultural Credit Conditions* deals with farm loans and interest rates.

68. Federal Reserve Bank of Kansas City. *Annual Report.* Kansas City, MO. Annual.
The Tenth Federal Reserve District includes Colorado, Kansas, Nebraska, Oklahoma, and parts of Missouri and New Mexico. Its *Annual Report* includes financial statements of income, expenses, conditions, and volume of principal operations. The *Monthly Review* is issued ten times a year and deals with national and regional economic and financial developments. The monthly *Financial Letter* summarizes financial activity of banks in the district. Data include deposits by type, loans, investments, and reports of condition. A companion publication, *Tenth District Depository Institutions and Large Commercial Bank Statistics,* reports on the monthly financial activities of financial institutions in the district.

69. Federal Reserve Bank of Minneapolis. *Annual Report.* Minneapolis, MN. Annual.
The Ninth Federal Reserve District includes Minnesota, Montana, North Dakota, South Dakota, and parts of Michigan and Wisconsin. The *Annual Report* gives assets, liabilities, earnings, and expenses for the bank. The *Quarterly Review* deals with financial and economic topics of national and regional significance. Another quarterly, *Agricultural Credit Conditions Survey,* analyzes farm debt, loan demand by farmers, debt refinancing, and short-term interest rate trends. A companion quarterly, *District Economic Conditions,* includes financial indicators such as commercial bank loans by type, deposits at banking institutions, and their assets and liabilities.

70. Federal Reserve Bank of New York. *Annual Report.* New York, NY. Annual.
The Second Federal Reserve District includes New York, Puerto Rico, the Virgin Islands, and parts of New Jersey and Connecticut. The *Annual Report* analyzes international financial developments and reviews the earnings, expenses, assets, and liabilities of the district banks. The *Quarterly Review* analyzes domestic and international financial issues, and reports on Treasury and Federal Reserve foreign exchange operations, Federal Reserve monetary policy, and Federal Reserve open market operations.

16 *A Guide to Statistical Sources in Money, Banking, and Finance*

71. Federal Reserve Bank of Philadelphia. *Annual Report.* Philadelphia, PA. Annual.
The Third Federal Reserve District includes Delaware and parts of New Jersey and Pennsylvania. The *Annual Report* presents financial statements of income, expenses, condition, and volume of principal operations. The bimonthly *Business Review* deals with Federal Reserve policies and operations as well as economic and financial developments which affect the Third District.

72. Federal Reserve Bank of Richmond. *Annual Report.* Richmond, VA. Annual.
The Fifth Federal Reserve District includes Maryland, North Carolina, South Carolina, Virginia, the District of Columbia, and part of West Virginia. The *Annual Report* details the bank's operations, financial condition, earnings, and expenses. The bimonthly *Economic Review* deals with financial and economic developments in the district. Its annual *Business Forecasts* summarizes forecasts from private and government sources. Its quarterly *Consolidated Reports of Condition and Income* deals with the operations of insured commercial banks in the district arranged by state and size. It contains some of the data included in a discontinued publication, *Income and Expenses: Member Banks and Foreign and Domestic Subsidiaries in the Fifth Federal Reserve District.* Another quarterly, *Cross Sections,* reviews business and economic conditions in the district and includes financial indicators such as bank deposits and loan activity by type of loan. The district's agricultural financial situation is dealt with in the quarterly *Farm Credit Conditions in the Fifth District.*

73. Federal Reserve Bank of San Francisco. *Annual Report.* San Francisco, CA. Annual.
The Twelfth Federal Reserve District includes Alaska, Arizona, California, Guam, Hawaii, Idaho, Nevada, Oregon, Utah, and Washington. The *Annual Report* contains a description of banking activity in the district as well as a statement of financial conditions. Some of the commercial banking data were covered in a now discontinued quarterly, *Western Economic Indicators.* A review of national and regional economic development is available in the quarterly *Economic Review.*

74. Federal Reserve Bank of St. Louis. *Annual Report.* St. Louis, MO. Annual.
The Eighth Federal Reserve District includes Arkansas and parts of Illinois, Indiana, Kentucky, Mississippi, Missouri, and Tennessee. The *Annual Report* details the bank's operation, financial condition, earnings, and expenses. The *Review,* published ten times a year, deals with U.S. economic and financial developments. The monthly *National Economic Trends* provides economic and financial statistics on various aspects of the nation's economy. The quarterly *International Economic Conditions* is a compilation of data on foreign exchange rates, international transactions, money supply, the Eurocurrency market, and other topics. A companion publication, *Annual U.S. Economic Data,* provides annual rates of change for selected monetary and economic indicators, such as money supply and reserves, currency component of money stop measures, and commercial bank deposits. Farm finance conditions in the Eighth District are dealt with in a quarterly, *Agriculture: An Eighth*

District Perspective, which provides information on farm credits, interest rates, and loan losses and delinquencies. The quarterly *Banking and Finance: An Eighth District Perspective* gives a summary of financial conditions affecting the banks in the Eighth District. It includes data on bank assets and liabilities, performance ratios, interest paid on NOW accounts, money market deposit accounts, and certificates of deposit. Data are shown in some cases by bank size.

75. Northwestern Banker. *Iowa-Nebraska Bank Directory.* Des Moines, IA. Annual.

Summarizes the financial condition of banks in the two states and lists bank executives.

76. Shawmut Bank of Boston. *Bank Directory of New England.* Boston, MA. Annual.

Contains summary statements of the financial condition of commercial banks and their branches. Includes a directory of executives.

77. Western Banker Publications. *Western Bank Directory.* Boise, ID, 1950– . Annual.

Provides financial and related information on commercial banking institutions in Alaska, Arizona, California, Hawaii, Idaho, Montana, Nevada, New Mexico, Oregon, Utah, Washington, and Wyoming.

National Sources

78. Advertising News Research. *Bank Rate Monitor.* Miami Beach, FL. Weekly.
   Provides information on money market account interest rates in the nation's top 75 financial markets.

79. American Banker Inc. *American Banker.* New York, NY. 5 issues/wk.
   Contains news trends and data on the banking industry. Statistical tables include rankings of top banks and trust companies, foreign banks in the U.S., insured commercial banks, thrifts, and correspondent banks. Data on the banks cover loans, assets, deposits, credit balances, demand deposits, savings, asset value, net worth, equity capital, profitability and performance ratios, and growth rates.

80. American Bankers Association. *ABA Bank Card Letter.* Washington, DC. Monthly.
   Newsletter covering the credit card industry in general and bank cards in particular. Contains some statistical data on the industry. Also summarizes results of surveys conducted by other agencies. Reports the most important findings relating to industry trends.

81. ——. *Confidential Bank Insurance Survey.* Washington, DC. Annual.
   Provides the results of a survey establishing a current profile of bank insurance, arranged by bank size. Data include coverage by type of policy, blanket bond coverage, premiums by type and deposit size of the bank, and loss experience by selected types, such as check fraud, robbery, and employee dishonesty.

82. ——. *Consumer Credit Delinquency Bulletin.* Washington, DC. Quarterly.
   A loan is considered delinquent if a payment is more than 30 days overdue. Provides data on the ratio of delinquent loans to outstanding loans and on the repossession ratios for automobiles and mobile homes. Includes delinquency information for loans by type, such as personal, home appliance, property improvement, recreational vehicle, bank credit card, and revolving credit loans. Prior to 1984 the report was entitled *Delinquency Rates on Bank Installment Loans.*

83. ———. *Delinquency Rates on Bank Installment Loans.* Washington, DC. Quarterly.

Monthly delinquency rates are collected and issued quarterly for installment loans, including such classes as personal, home appliance, automobile direct and indirect, mobile home, recreational vehicle, and property improvement loans. These categories are then combined into a weighted average and computed on both a national and state-by-state basis. There are also separate statistics for bank card and revolving credit loans. The repossession ratios per 1,000 loans for automobiles and mobile homes are also reported state by state.

84. ———. *Installment/Consumer Credit Report.* Washington, DC. Annual.

Compiled from questionnaires mailed to a representative nationwide sample of U.S. banks, this publication provides statistics for evaluating bank installment loan programs. Data include installment credit outstanding as a percentage of total deposits, income, expenses, cost of funds, loan losses, extended term automobile financing, simple interest loans, auto leasing, and credit cards. The amount of savings and interest computation on passbook savings accounts are also included.

85. ———. *NACHA (National Automated Clearing House Association) Sure Pay Update.* Washington, DC. Bimonthly.

Newsletter on current activities of automated clearing houses. Presents the latest developments in sure pay and electronic payment services made possible by regional automated clearing houses. Each issue gives statistical data regarding transaction volume, including private debits and credits and government credits. An update is provided on the participation of bank membership and thrift membership and the number of companies belonging to local clearing houses.

86. ———. *Retail Bank Credit Report.* Washington, DC, 1960– . Annual.

Covers bank retail lending activity, by asset size and census division, in terms of installment credit, bank cards, other types of lending, overdraft line of credit, and credit life insurance. Selected data include installment credit outstanding by type of loan and/or lender, banks' ratios of total loans to total assets and of consumer loans to total loans, portfolio distribution of loan volume and loans outstanding by type of loan, average number of accounts per bank in open-end credit plans, installment credit dollar losses based on liquidations and volume, portfolio distribution of losses and recoveries, average number of automobiles repossessed, and average number of delinquent loans per month.

87. American Financial Services Association. *Finance Facts Yearbook.* Washington, DC, 1961– . Annual.

Reports on consumer finance industry lending activity and financial status and on consumer income and expenditures, including savings and debt. Also includes data on the status of industrial banking companies. Data are derived from responses to a survey of finance companies and from the Federal Reserve Board. Among other categories, information on the following is provided: consumer income; spending; capital formation; sources and disposition of personal income; selected income characteristics of households, families, and unrelated individuals, by total income;

personal income, by source, and its disposition, by object; capital formation; capital consumption allowances; consumer savings, investment, and debt; total credit market debt owed, by sector (public, private, and consumer); consumer credit, including commercial banks, retailers, gasoline and finance companies, savings and loans, credit unions, and mutual savings banks. Installment credit is shown for automobile financing, revolving charges, and mobile home purchase loans. Consumer finance industry operations are described in terms of lending activity.

88. Association of Bank Holding Companies. *Bank Holding Company Facts.* Washington, DC, 1958– . Semiannual.

Provides comprehensive financial data on companies registered with the Federal Reserve Board under the Bank Holding Companies Act of 1956. Includes a ranking of bank holding companies by deposit sizes, assets, and state.

89. Bank Administration Institute. *Analysis of Bank Marketing Expenditures.* Rolling Meadows, IL. Annual.

A study of how bank marketers spent their budgets, on which media and on which basic services. Covers advertising, public relations, sales promotion, sales/customer relations training, marketing research, allocation of nonsalary marketing expenditures, how banks use outside agencies, and how they are compensated. Information is for the whole marketing industry, not just the Institute's members. Covers expenditures on marketing of debit cards, telephone bill paying, NOW accounts, and credit card duality. Includes a special section on direct mail.

90. ———. *ATM Cost Model.* Rolling Meadows, IL, 1983– . Annual.

This publication provides the results of a survey of fully weighted and incremental automatic teller machine transaction costs, presented in 20 charts. Includes cost figures for different types of ATM transactions.

91. ———. *ATM Directory.* Rolling Meadows, IL. Annual.

Issued as a special number of the *Magazine of Bank Administration*, this comprehensive guide provides facts relating to automated teller machine services. The directory lists more than 600 products and services of 400 companies offering ATM-related hardware, software, and peripherals, and consultants, graphics, maintenance, and turnkey services.

92. ———. *Bank Officer Cash Compensation Survey.* Rolling Meadows, IL, 1973– . Annual.

Provides information on bank employees' salaries, bank asset size, and census division. Includes mean and median base salaries, salary range, number of reporting banks, and incumbents for officer level and other positions. Also includes officers' mean age, years of service, employees supervised, and salary comparisons.

93. ———. *Index of Bank Performance.* Rolling Meadows, IL, 1973– . Annual.

This is the banking industry's first comparative index for evaluating bank performance. Provides a method for measuring a bank's performance against that of other banks of equal size, within state boundaries, in a specific market area, or against the industry as a whole. The *Index* is based on the universal call report and income statement tapes generated by the federal banking agencies. Therefore, the database includes all insured commercial banks in the U.S. Throughout the current report 46 ratios are used consistently, and the method used to develop the ratios is defined. In general, the ratios measure operating performance, yields and rates, loan loss data, balance sheet data, and growth rates.

94. ———. *Individual Bank Profiles.* Park Ridge, IL. Annual.

To be used as a supplement to the *Index of Bank Performance*, this publication shows the following ratios: loan types as a percent of average loans, deposit as a percent of average total deposits, trust income as a percent of assets, and service charges on deposit accounts.

95. ———. *Plastic Card Float Study.* Rolling Meadows, IL, 1986– . (Irregular).

Focuses on the float costs associated with plastic card transaction processing. Analyzes various types of plastic card transactions, such as credit and debit card purchases and automatic teller machine deposits, withdrawals, and cash advances.

96. ———. *Survey of the Check Collection System.* Rolling Meadows, IL, 1971– . Annual.

Deals with the performance of the banking industry's check collection system. Provides a general set of measures for evaluating check processing operations. These include average reject rate, transit holdover, transit return items, employee productivity, check safekeeping, and electronic presentment. The data provided enable comparison of an individual bank's experiences with peer institutions.

97. ———. *Survey of the Electronic Funds Transfer Transaction System.* Rolling Meadows, IL, 1979– . Annual.

This study concentrates on three electronic funds transfer services: ACH, ATM, and POS. It analyzes the growth usage pattern and transaction mix of each. Also available is an annual companion publication, *Funds Transfer Bank Contact Directory*, which contains the names and telephone numbers of bankers responsible for funds transfer operations around the country. It reports on the banking industry's use of electronic funds transfer and automated clearing houses, which move debit and credit transactions among financial institutions and automated teller machines. The report arranges data by major city and region. The ATM transaction types include cash withdrawals from credit cards, checking and savings deposits, and bill payments. Point of sale locations include main offices, branches, and off-premises. Installation types include lobby, vestibule, through-the-wall, drive-up, free standing, shopping center, and hospital.

98. ———. *U.S. Bank Performance Profile.* Rolling Meadows, IL, 1973– . Annual.

Presents financial and operating performance ratios for banks, by size and state. Operating performance ratios include interest and noninterest income, expenses, salaries/benefits, and return on assets and equity, all expressed as percent of total assets. Other data include yields and rates, capital position, productivity, and assets/liability management in terms of sources and uses of funds. Customized analyses of operating ratios for individual banks or groups of banks are also available.

99. Bankcard Holders of America. *Bankcard Consumer News*. Washington, DC. Quarterly.
> Contains data on terms of credit extended and interest rates charged by banks on consumer credit cards.

100. Banker's Desk Reference. *Banker's Desk Reference*. Boston, MA, 1978– . Annual.
> This is an instant pocket reference book of financial information and banks in the U.S.

101. Banker's Research Inc. *Banker's Research*. Westport, CT, 1946– . Semimonthly.
> Deals with important trends and developments in the following areas: mortgage market, consumer installment credit, and savings and demand deposits. Statistical data on these areas are available in most issues.

102. Bankers Trust Co. *Credit and Capital Markets*. New York, NY. Annual.
> Reports on credit and capital formation activities in short-term and long-term financial markets, including analyses of the sources and uses of funds raised through corporate, government, and financial instruments of credit. Also discusses activities of financial institutions, insurance companies, pension funds, and investment companies. Data on the following are included: funds raised by type of marketable instrument and funds supplied by institutions, government, and foreign and individual investors. A special section covers foreign activity in U.S. credit and capital markets.

103. Chicago Board of Trade. *Interest Rate and Metals Futures Statistical Annual*. Chicago, IL, 1982– . Annual.
> This is a compilation of statistics on futures trading in fixed interest rate securities and precious metals on the Chicago Board of Trade. Covers depository receipts, certificates of deposit, long-term Treasury bonds, Treasury bond options, Treasury notes, domestic certificates of deposit, gold, and silver. For each category high, low, and closing prices; sales volume; and monthly price range are given.

104. Chicago Mercantile Exchange. *International Monetary Market Yearbook*. Chicago, IL, 1979– . Annual.
> Provides information on International Monetary Market futures trading in gold, U.S. silver coins, Treasury bills and notes, certificates of deposit, foreign currencies, and Eurodollar time deposits. Includes data on trading volume, price trends, daily price ranges, settlement prices, and open interest. Information is also given on market yields and price ranges, Federal Reserve interest rates, open market operations, and money market rates.

105. Commodity Exchange Inc. *COMEX Statistical Yearbook*. New York, NY, 1978– . Annual.
> Reports on the futures trading activity at the commodity exchange for gold, silver, copper, and gold options. Shows opening, high, low, closing, and settlement prices; trading volume; open interest; depository stocks; and deliveries by trading day and delivery month. Also includes metal

prices showing London bullion fixing and Handy and Harman base price for silver.

106. Communication Channels Inc. *Directory of Trust Institutions.* Atlanta, GA, 1962– . Annual.

This is a detailed guide to American and Canadian banking trust companies and their branches. Includes financial data as well as information on financial executives.

107. The Conference Board. *Financial Indicators and Corporate Financing Plans.* New York, NY. 1976– . Semiannual.

Deals with corporate financial executives' planned sources of corporate financing: bond issues, private placements, net new equity, long-term and short-term loans, commercial paper, and other external sources as well as internal funds. Includes data on foreign exchange rate changes for four major currencies against the U.S. dollar and changes in the price of gold.

108. Conference of State Bank Supervisors. *Profile of State Chartered Banking.* Washington, DC, 1967– . Biennial.

Contains financial and related data on the operation of chartered banks in each state.

109. Credit Union National Association. *Credit Union Report.* Madison, WI. Annual.

Covers credit union finances, operations, and trends. Selected data arranged by state include the following: total number of credit unions, membership, value of shares/deposits, outstanding loans, reserves, assets, credit union distribution, types of services offered, operating ratios, types of charters, savings, loans, reserves, assets, share drafts, individual retirement accounts, and money market accounts. Also included is information on installment and automobile loans as well as interest rates by type of loan.

110. ———. *CUNA Yearbook.* Madison, WI. Annual.

Provides statistics on the activities of state-chartered and federal credit unions, including number of members, savings shares, deposits, median savings, outstanding loans, reserves, assets, and operating data.

111. Crittenden Publishing Inc. *The Crittenden Directory.* Novato, CA. Annual.

Lists every major national lender, investor, and joint venturer plus many major local lenders and their assets, loan portfolios, the prior year's commitments by type of loan, types of financing, types of projects, and geographical investing areas. It includes the names, addresses, and phone numbers of the persons to contact. For easy reference, the *Directory* is indexed by type of investment for all financial institutions. Types of loans include construction and interim, commercial, office building, foreign money, joint venture, equity, industrial, medical, apartment, and special purpose.

112. ———. *The Crittenden Report.* Novato, CA. Annual.

Contains useful information about real estate financing concentrated in just four pages. Includes information on commercial banks, savings and loans, life insurance companies, syndicators, stockbrokers, pension funds, and credit companies.

113. Cyrus J. Lawrence, Inc. *Weekly Money Report.* New York, NY, 1982– . Weekly.
Deals with money supply, interest rates, and other monetary and credit information as reported by the Federal Reserve Board.

114. Dun and Bradstreet. *Monthly Bank Clearings.* New York, NY. Monthly.
Reports on bank check clearings in New York City and 25 other major cities in the country. Compares bank clearings by city.

115. Ernst and Whinney. *Financial Reporting Trends: Banking.* New York, NY. Annual.
Surveys banking industry reporting practices, as revealed in annual reports selected from among the 500 largest banks in the U.S. The findings are presented in three categories: commercial banks, multibank holding companies, and single-bank holding companies. Among the subjects surveyed are statistical disclosures, statements of condition, and statements of income. Also summarizes prevailing accounting practices. In addition, examples from the individual reporting banks that illustrate either representative or unusual reporting practices are provided, as are analyses of annual reports on Form 10-K filed with the Securities and Exchange Commission.

116. Federal Deposit Insurance Corporation. *Bank Operating Statistics.* Washington, DC. Annual.
This is a very detailed report on the number and financial condition of all FDIC-insured banks based on reports of condition and income. Data include: consolidated financial statements detailing assets, liabilities, equity capital, income, and expenses for ratio analysis. Also includes data on domestic and foreign branches. This lengthy report was discontinued after 1983. Its coverage is continued by the Federal Financial Institutions Examination Council's *Uniform Bank Performance Report.*

117. ———. *Data Book: Operating Banks and Branches.* Washington, DC. Annual.
Contains a summary of deposits in all commercial and mutual savings banks and domestic branches of foreign banks. Information is arranged by type of account for all states, including Washington, DC, and individual outlying areas, counties, SMSAs, and individual banks and branches. The report was issued irregularly before 1980. It usually has about 20 volumes.

118. ———. *FDIC Annual Report.* Washington, DC. Annual.
The Corporation has regulatory jurisdiction over all U.S. commercial and mutual savings banks. The annual report provides a detailed summary of activities relating to bank supervision, bank mergers, depositors' protection, and enforcement activities. Data include statistics on the total resources and deposits of banks affected by merger decisions, number of bank absorptions, comparative statements of financial position, income and the deposit insurance fund of the FDIC, amount of deposit insurance disbursed because of bank closings, and the names and locations of failing institutions.

119. Federal Financial Institutions Examination Council. *Bank Holding Company Performance Report.* Washington, DC, 1985– . Semiannual.

Published in the same format as *Uniform Bank Performance Report*, this report contains balance sheet and income data as well as performance ratios which enable detailed financial analysis of bank holding companies. The report contains consolidated and parent company data for bank holding companies arranged by asset size.

120. ———. *Country Exposure Lending Survey.* Washington, DC. Quarterly.

Statistical release on foreign lending by domestic and foreign branches of U.S. banks. Data are from a quarterly survey of 198 banks with significant foreign banking operations. Survey covers lending from a bank's offices in one country to residents of another country or lending in a currency other than that of the borrower. All data are shown by country with totals for Group of Ten and other developed countries, Eastern Europe, OPEC members, non-oil exporting developing countries by world region, off-shore banking centers, and international and regional organizations. Includes amounts owed to U.S. banks by foreign borrowers and cross-border and nonlocal currency contingent claims.

121. ———. *Uniform Bank Performance Report.* Washington, DC, 1981– . Annual with quarterly updates.

Available in two parts: *State Average Report* and *Peer Group Report*. Both provide balance sheet and income data as well as performance ratios which enable financial analysis of all insured commercial banks. This publication continues the Federal Deposit Insurance Corporation's *Bank Operating Statistics*, discontinued in 1984.

122. Federal Home Loan Bank Board. *Annual Report.* Washington, DC. Annual.

Covers activities and financial performance of the Federal Home Loan Bank Board, Federal Savings and Loan Insurance Corporation, and Federal Home Loan Mortgage Corporation as well as the savings institutions doing business under the system. Data include the number of institutions, sources and uses of funds, assets and liabilities, statements of condition, income, expenses, and retained earnings as well as some statistics on the housing market.

123. ———. *Asset and Liability Trends.* Washington, DC. Annual.

Provides information on the assets, liabilities, and capital accounts of savings and loans. Financial details include mortgages and other loans, investments, real estate holdings, and net worth. Data are given by type of association, i.e., whether federal or state chartered or uninsured.

124. ———. *Combined Financial Statements.* Washington, DC. Annual.

Provides data on the balance sheet and income and expense statements of FSLIC-insured savings institutions. Financial ratio items include income, expenses, assets, liabilities, taxes, net worth, and outstanding loans by types.

125. ───── *Conventional Home Mortgage Rates.* Washington, DC. Monthly.

Provides loan commitment and loan closing interest rates, loan-to-price ratio, and other terms for conventional single-family home mortgages. Includes data on the type of lender; type of loan, i.e., whether fixed rate or adjustable; and mortgage purpose, i.e., whether new home, existing home, or combined construction home. Loan terms include interest rate, fees and charges, maturity term, loan amount, and purchase price. National average interest rates as well as actual interests for large metropolitan areas are supplied.

126. ─────. *Journal.* Washington, DC. Monthly.

Contains a series of statistical data relating to money supply, security yields and trades, mortgage loans, interest rates, savings and loans, and housing markets. In 1985, the *Journal* was superceded by a monthly entitled *The Outlook*.

127. ─────. *News.* Washington, DC. Monthly.

Presents operating and financial data for Federal Home Loan Banks. Includes information on statements of condition, interest rates and lending activity, outstanding loans, and consolidated obligations.

128. ─────. *Savings and Home Financing Sourcebook.* Washington, DC. Annual.

Reports on the savings and loan industry's deposits, mortgage lending activity, assets, and liabilities. Includes data on selected balance sheet items, savings, mortgage purchases and debts, loan commitments, foreclosures, delinquencies, and the general financial condition of the industry. Covers cost of funds as well as sources and uses.

129. ─────. *Summary of Savings by Geographic Area.* Washington, DC. Annual.

Deals with savings accounts at FSLIC insured savings institutions. Savings balances are given in the following breakdown: U.S. totals, home loan bank districts, states, SMSAs, and counties.

130. ─────. *Thrift Institution Activity.* Washington, DC. Monthly.

This is a statistical release on deposits, loans, assets, and liabilities of insured savings institutions. Data include mortgage loans and construction loans for residential structures and consumer and commercial loans.

131. Federal Home Loan Mortgage Corporation. *Freddie Mac Reports.* Washington, DC, 1983– . Monthly.

Provides statistics on secondary mortgage markets.

132. Federal Reserve Bank of St. Louis. *Monetary Trends.* St. Louis, MO. Monthly.

Includes charts and statistical tables showing the monetary trends for the country. Specific data cover money supply, commercial bank deposits, monetary and reserve base, bank loans and investments, federal budget trends, and trends for selected long-term interest rates and money market rates. For each of these items compounded annual rates of change are supplied.

133. ———. *U.S. Financial Data.* St. Louis, MO. Weekly.
This is a compilation of charts and tables relating to current financial and monetary indicators. Compounded annual rates of change are provided for the monetary base, money stock, money multiplier and currency component of money stock, total deposit, yields on selected securities, selected interest rates, money market accounts, money market mutual fund balances, and super NOW accounts.

134. Federally Insured Financial Institutions. *Bank Crime Statistics.* Washington, DC. Semiannual.
Provides comprehensive statistics on crimes against financial institutions: robberies, burglaries, larcenies, and Hobbs Act violations. The occurrences are reported by state including the amount involved, recoveries if any, and securities devices utilized. Bank frauds and embezzlements are dealt with according to the type of financial institution.

135. Financial Economist Publications. *Financial Economist.* Bala Cynwyd, PA, 1983– . Monthly.
Published in two editions, national and international, this monthly covers key financial indicators, such as money supply and interest rates. Contains detailed and informative charts as well as tabular data on foreign exchange rates, inflation rates, yield movements, and prices of important commodities like gold.

136. Financial Publishing. *Cost of Personal Borrowing in the United States.* Boston, MA, 1971– . Annual.
Provides data on maximum legal interest rates on installment credit in all the states.

137. First National Bank of Chicago. *Consumer Finance (Direct Cash Lending) Company Ratios.* Chicago, IL, 1948– . Annual.
Presents aggregate lending ratios and other financial data for consumer finance companies involved in direct cash lending. It is based on a survey of national and regional loan companies conducted by Robert Morris Associates. The report shows data on lending volume, loan amount outstanding, average loan size and balance, and delinquency rates.

138. ———. *Diversified Finance Company Ratios.* Chicago, IL, 1935– . Annual.
Presents aggregate lending ratios and other financial data for national and regional diversified finance companies. The report is based on a survey conducted by Robert Morris Associates. It includes data on annual lending volume and loans outstanding and has an analysis of retail automobile finance.

139. ———. *Ratios of the Installment Sales Finance and Consumer Finance Corporation.* Chicago, IL. Semiannual.
To assist those who are interested in the trends and financial stability of the finance company industry, the First National Bank of Chicago has published composite financial ratios for the industry for many years. Data for sales finance companies has been compiled since 1935 and for consumer finance companies since 1948. A total of 53 ratios is available for installment sales finance companies and 35 for consumer finance.

Each report covers the previous three and one-half years, divided into six-month periods. In November 1978, a pamphlet explaining all the ratios was prepared by J. Russell Hanson of the First National Bank of Chicago.

140. Friedman, Milton, and Schwartz, A. J. *Monetary Statistics of the United States.* New York: National Bureau of Economic Research, 1970. 629p.

Provides historical data on money stock measures such as currency, deposits, bank vault cash, and gold.

141. Futures Industry Association. *Volume of Futures Trading.* Washington, DC, 1985– . Annual.

Reports on volume of futures trading for securities, commodities, and foreign currencies, by commodity and exchange, with detailed and summary trends. Also includes options traded. Supplemented by the *Monthly Volume Report: Futures Contracts Traded*, a weekly bulletin on volume of futures traded on approximately ten exchanges, arranged by commodity and exchange.

142. Golemba Associates. *Bank Expansion Quarterly.* Washington, DC. Quarterly.

Provides detailed data on all bank acquisitions and mergers and other expansion activities.

143. Handy and Harman. *Silver Market: An Annual Review.* New York, NY, 1915– . Annual.

Reports on silver market activity in the U.S. and the non-communist world. Includes data on silver stocks, consumption by end use, foreign trade, and prices. High, low, and average daily London fixes and New York prices are included. End-use data cover industrial uses and coinage.

144. HSN Consultants. *The Nilson Report.* Los Angeles, CA. Semimonthly.

Newsletter providing current information on all credit card operations. Statistical information on Mastercard and Visa operations appears periodically. The data include number of participating banks, active accounts, and the total dollar volume transacted. Frequently data are broken down by travel and entertainment, retail, and oil company credit card transactions. Also includes information on travelers' checks, plastic card suppliers, check cashing systems, card embossers, and credit card protection services.

145. Institutional Investor. *Bank Letter.* New York, NY. Weekly.

Review of important news about people and events in commercial banking. It covers new developments in retail banking and corporate lending, including the changing relationship between banks and their corporate clients. Also reports legislative and regulatory developments, what fees are being charged, and what bankers think will happen to interest rates.

146. Investment Company Institute. *Trends in Mutual Fund Activity.* Washington, DC. Monthly.

Presents statistics on mutual fund sales, assets, and investments, by investment objective.

147. Irving Trust Co. *Financial Markets Weekly.* New York, NY. Weekly.

Report on financial market conditions. Supplements the monthly *Economic Outlook*, which analyzes major business, industrial, and government economic performance indicators. The weekly tables include prime interest rate, discount rate, market yields for federal funds, Treasury issues, negotiable certificates of deposit, banker's acceptances, Eurodollar deposits, and prime commercial paper.

148. Manufacturers Hanover Trust. *Financial Digest.* New York, NY. Weekly.

Reports on trends and activities relating to money and securities markets. Data include information on interest rates and banking activities, selected Federal Reserve transactions, New York money market trends, short-term paper outstanding, certificates of deposit, commercial paper, commercial and industrial bank loans, and Eurodollar and foreign exchange rates. Supplements the bank's companion monthly, *Economic Report*, which also includes selected financial and monetary indicators.

149. McFadden Business Publications. *American Bank Directory.* Norcross, GA, 1836– . Semiannual.

Provides summary information on the financial condition of commercial banks, based on balance sheets and income statements. Lists bank officers, directors, and branch offices.

150. ―――. *American Savings Directory.* Norcross, GA, 1982– . Annual.

Reports assets, liabilities, and other financial data on savings and loans, credit unions, mutual savings banks, and money market funds. Lists bank officers and directors.

151. ―――. *Directory of American Financial Institutions.* Norcross, GA, 1836– . Annual.

Provides statistical and related information on all financial institutions in the country. Covers most of the commercial and savings banks included in the *American Bank Directory* and *American Savings Directory*, listed above.

152. McGraw-Hill Economics Department. *U.S. Business Outlook: Short Term.* New York, NY. Quarterly.

This is an analysis of factors affecting the general business climate and the expected performance of the economy in the short term. Includes data on capital investment, fiscal and monetary policies, Treasury bill rates, corporate bond yields, consumer spending, and savings.

153. Moody's Investors Service. *Moody's Bank and Financial Manual.* New York, NY, 1928– . Annual.

Provides financial, operating, and related information on over 6,000 banks, trust companies, bank holding companies, and finance companies. The annual is updated by the weekly *News Reports*.

154. Mortgage Bankers Association of America. *Financial Statements and Operating Ratios for the Mortgage Banking Industry.* Washington, DC, 1964– . Annual.

Presents mortgage banking industry aggregate financial and operating data covering income, expenses, assets, liabilities, and selected activity indicators by volume and type of lending activity and type of ownership. Data are based on the Association's survey of member banks and enable individual banks to compare their performance with peers. Reports include mortgage loans closed and serviced; ownership, income statement, and balance sheet; and selected ratios, such as profitability, leverage, operating, and liquidity.

155. ———. *Loans Closed and Servicing Volume for the Mortgage Banking Industry.* Washington, DC, 1976– . Annual.

Reports on loans closed and serviced in the mortgage banking industry. Data are arranged by type of loan, investor, service, and origination volume. Investor institutions include life insurance companies, mutual savings banks, commercial banks, savings and loans, and state and federal agencies. Categories are total mortgage originations, average loan size, and loans closed and serviced.

156. ———. *Mortgage Banking.* Washington, DC, 1949– . Monthly.

Contains data on mortgage market trends and developments, including real estate investment and management, institutional lending, and profiles of prominent executives. Statistics include interest rates for new and existing mortgages, yields and point spreads, long-term loan activity, mortgage insurance, secondary mortgage market activity, and mortgage loan servicing.

157. ———. *Mortgage Banking Activity.* Washington, DC. Monthly.

Newsletter on activity in loans closed, commitments to builders and borrowers for long-term mortgages and land and construction loans, commitments from investors for long-term mortgages, mortgage servicing, long-term mortgages sold and purchased, and construction loans closed. Data serve as a barometer of mortgage banking activity.

158. ———. *Mortgage Banking Financial Statements and Operating Ratios.* Washington, DC. Annual.

Survey of members of the Mortgage Bankers Association. Provides mortgage bankers with composite average earning statements, balance sheets, operating ratios, and other key performance indicators. The tables show sources of income, increases in gross operating expense, experience on nonearning assets, an average mortgage inventory, personnel costs, and overall profitability. The ratios enable management to evaluate its performance in cost control and take steps to improve operating efficiency in specific areas.

159. The ———. *Mortgage Banking Loans Closed and Servicing Volume.* Washington, DC. Annual.

Survey of the Mortgage Bankers Association that provides detailed statistics on loan originations and servicing by types of loans and by types of investors. Year-to-year comparisons show changes in composition of the industry, loan servicing portfolio, and loan origination activity.

160. ——. *Mortgage Banking Survey of Single-Family Loan Operations.* Washington, DC. Annual.

Provides an extensive analysis of income and costs for originating and servicing single-family loans. Tables furnish data on the impact of slow or fast growth, the relation of high or low proportion of single-family activity in overall operations of the firm, different measures of size, the nature of single-family loans originated, and geographic breakdowns. A highlights section summarizes the data and indicates industry trends.

161. ——. *National Delinquency Survey.* Washington, DC. Quarterly.

Reports on residential mortgage loans with overdue installments by state for conventional, VA, and FHA loans. It is based on a survey of nearly 500 financial institutions. Tables show percent of loans 30, 60, 90 or more days delinquent and percent foreclosed.

162. National Association of Mutual Savings Banks. *Factbook.* New York, NY. Annual.

Comprehensive guide to the mutual savings bank industry providing current and historical data on assets; liabilities; deposits, including NOW accounts; mortgage loans; income; expenses; rates of return; and securities holdings. Data on trends in savings deposits, mortgage lending, and bank liquidity are also available in the Association's *Annual Report*, (1957–). Updated data on most of the above are available from the Association's monthly *The Savings Bank Journal*.

163. ——. *Mutual Savings Banking.* New York, NY, 1958– . Annual.

Provides statistical analysis of the performance of mutual savings banks during the report year as well as historical data.

164. National Consumer Finance Association. *NCFA Research Report on Finance Companies.* Washington, DC. Annual.

Information from surveys of consumer finance and sales finance companies which are members of the National Consumer Finance Association. The information is divided into three sections: five-year industry trends, consumer finance industry data, and comparative data by type and size of company. Section 1, industry trends, includes data on diversification of assets, sources of funds and income, current borrowing as a percent of bank lines, rates of interest on bank loans, size of loans, frequency of payment, charge-offs, and maturities of receivables. Section 2, consumer finance industry data, has aggregate data with detailed information on personal loans by number and size and by age, occupation, and income of the borrower. Section 3 lists selected averages and percentages by type of finance company. It is a very useful publication for ratio analysis and comparative performance.

165. National Council of Savings Institutions. *Directory.* Washington, DC. Annual.

Lists the Council's 600 members, which comprise over 40% of the nation's savings industries. Listings include officers and key personnel by function; form of ownership; type of insurance held, i.e., whether FDIC, FSLIC, or state; assets and deposits as of the last fiscal year; associate membership in the Council; international affiliates; directory of regional trade and state organizations; and a ranking of member institutions by asset size.

166. ———. *National Fact Book of Savings Institutions.* Washington, DC, 1960– . Annual.
Covers the financial condition and operations of savings institutions arranged by state, selected comparisons to other types of financial institutions; and trends. Contains the following composite financial data: assets and liabilities of savings institutions; deposit activity, savings, and time accounts in selected types of financial institutions, by type of account; financial savings by households; mortgage activity by savings institutions; institutional mortgage investment; mortgage delinquency rates and foreclosures; amounts held in retirement accounts in savings banks; ranking of top 100 thrift institutions in the U.S. in order of assets; rates of return on assets; and average annual rates of interest.

167. National Credit Union Administration. *Annual Report.* Washington, DC. Annual.
Provides detailed statistical data on federal credit unions and federally insured state credit unions. Information is arranged by state and region in the following areas: assets; liabilities; equity; income; expenses; loans, charge-offs, and recoveries; dividends; interest refunds; share accounts; financial ratios and averages by asset size; the number of charters issued; and liquidations.

168. ———. *State Chartered Credit Unions: Annual Report.* Washington, DC. Annual.
This is a state-by-state analysis of credit union activities in terms of their total number, savings and loan activity, assets, liabilities, income, expenses, capital, and reserves. Includes a list of the 100 largest credit unions.

169. National Federation of Independent Business. *NFIB Quarterly Economic Report for Small Business.* Washington, DC. Quarterly.
Report on the expectations of small business firms concerning economic conditions affecting their own businesses and business in general. Includes credit conditions and accounts receivable, including interest rates on short-term loans; interest rate and loan availability compared to prior quarter; expected credit availability for next quarter; and percent of accounts receivable due over 30 days.

170. National News Services. *Bank and Quotation Record.* Arlington, MA, 1927– . Monthly.
Data include stock quotations for banks and finance companies, call loan rates, certificates of deposit, commercial paper, federal funds, foreign exchange rates, prime banker's acceptances, and values for U.S. Government securities like short-term Treasury bills and long-term obligations.

171. New World Decisions. *Bank Credit Card Observer.* Iselin, NJ, 1986– . Monthly.
Highlights national bank credit card trends, reporting credit card interest rates, comparing different types of credit cards, providing a table showing each city's lowest to highest bank credit card rates, and ranking of annual bank percentage rates. Includes a monthly supplement, *Bank*

Credit Card Balances and Repayment Habits, which provides in-depth analysis of the credit card industry and consumer usage.

172. Olson Analytical Services. *Olson BancScore*. Greenbelt, MD, 1984– . Quarterly.

Gives the most current annual report and 10-K data for banking companies with assets over one billion dollars. It provides a three-year history and a projection for the current and following years. Financial highlights include rate of return, risk, and total performance scores for five years. Available in hard copy or on floppy disk to be used with Lotus 1-2-3.

173. Purcell, Graham. *Applied Economics for Card Systems*. By Jack W. Cox. New York, NY. Monthly.

Newsletter containing important and comprehensive data on the credit card industry. Articles report information on specific card issues with data for number of cardholders, charge volume, outstandings, net write-offs, and earnings. A "Card Trends" summary appears each month with statistics on total outstandings and extensions for bank cards and total card market. Columns on new products and services are included.

174. Rand McNally. *American Bankers Association Key to Routing Numbers*. Skokie, IL, 1911– . Annual.

Deals with check routing between financial institutions in the U.S. It is a numerical list with the check digit and alphabetical list of financial depository institutions in the U.S. showing routing numbers and special ABA identification numbers. It is also available on magnetic tape.

175. ———. Financial Publishing Division. *The Desktop Bank Directory*. Chicago, IL. Annual.

Contains data on banks arranged by city and state. Includes population, county, and Federal Reserve district, all in-city branch locations, names and locations of principal correspondents, holding company relationships, Federal Reserve membership, and routing number. Financial summary includes assets, loans, deposits, equity, and net income.

176. Robert Morris Associates. *Domestic and International Commercial Loan Charge-Offs*. Philadelphia, PA. Annual.

This report is based on an annual survey of the member banks of Robert Morris Associates. It provides detailed data on commercial loan charge-offs and is designed for evaluating a specific bank's performance. The domestic section includes gross charge-off, recovery, and net charge-off figures and indicates the distribution of charge-offs by number of loans and by dollars involved. Data are provided by bank asset size and by Federal Reserve district. High-loss industries are ranked, and a list of the top 20 high-loss industries anticipated for the coming year is included. The international section presents gross charge-off, recovery, and net charge-off data by bank size categories. It also indicates aggregate charge-off experience by country and by type of borrower.

177. Salomon Brothers. *Bank Analysts Quarterly Handbook.* New York, NY. Quarterly.
Provides the following key operating figures regarding large commercial banks: earnings, net income, return on assets, return on equity, income taxes, interest margin, loans, loan reserves, net charge-offs, and leverage.

178. ———. *Constant Prepayment Rate Yield Tables.* New York, NY, 1986. 3 vols.
Deals with the mortgage-backed securities for the Federal National Mortgage Association, Government National Mortgage Association, and Federal Home Loan Mortgage Corporation. Enables investors to determine the dollar price, yield, average life, and duration of mortgage securities for a full range of coupon rates and remaining terms at various constant prepayment rates for Ginnie Mae, Freddie Macs, and Fanny Maes.

179. ———. *A Review of Bank Performance.* New York, NY. Annual.
Provides overall performance rating of selected commercial banks in terms of profitability, credit quality, capital adequacy, productivity, liquidity, market price, book value, dividend yield, price-earnings ratios, and selected interstate banking comparisons.

180. Savers Advisory Service. *Jumbo Rate News.* Coral Gables, FL, 1984– . Weekly.
Reports the interest rates on large certificates of deposit in major markets around the U.S.

181. ———. *Saver's Rate News.* Coral Gables, FL, 1983– . Weekly.
Newsletter monitors interest rates for medium and small savers. Covers major U.S. markets.

182. Securities Industries Association. *Securities Industries Trends.* New York, NY. 8/yr.
This is an analysis of emerging trends in the securities industry. Each issue contains statistical tables on stock market activity, corporate and municipal bond yields, bond underwriting activity, and selected interest rates.

183. Sheshunoff & Co. *The Bank of Your State.* Austin, TX. Annual.
This publication, which enables comparisons of commercial banks by geographic area or peer groups, is available for every state in the union. Provides information which could be used in the financial evaluation of individual banks. Includes information like comparative balance sheet and income statement analysis, equity, loan activity, operating ratios, competitive analysis, and rankings by rate of return, deposit growth, and net worth. Each volume includes individual bank overviews within each state. An annual companion publication, *The S & L's of Your State*, provides similar information for savings and loans as well as composite financial information on profitability, yields, costs of funds, spreads, fee income, operating expenses, capital adequacy, performance analysis rankings and growth, and market share. The annual *The Bank Holding Companies of the United States* contains data for evaluating individual banks or entire holding companies in terms of loan quality, earnings, interest spreads, debt structure, capital adequacy, goodwill, deposit mix, dividend payouts, and tax position. The three key analysis sections

contained in the volume are the consolidated analysis, which includes comparative balance sheets and income statements for holding companies; parent company analysis; and multibank holding company subsidiary bank analysis. Two other publications, spin-offs from the above, are *The Bank Ratings of All US Banks* and *The S & L Ratings of All US Savings and Loans,* both annuals. The ratings guidelines are based on factors widely used by bank presidents and bank regulators: capital adequacy, asset quality, earnings, liquidity, loan growth, repossessed assets, nonperforming loans, and net charge-offs. The special analysis section covers issues related to bank safety and soundness. The *National Quarterly Ratings and Analysis Service* for both insured commercial banks and insured savings and loans provides updated information on each institution in regard to size, growth, rating, loan exposure, capital adequacy, asset quality, earnings, and liquidity. The publishers also provide a microcomputer banking software service which enables subscribers to analyze financial statements, rate sensitivity, safe deposit operations, and call report services and to price loans and bank services.

184. Silver Institute. *Silver Institute Letter: Information on Silver Industry.* Washington, DC, 1982– . Bimonthly.
Covers worldwide production of refined silver, its disposition, and stocks. Includes data on average price of silver and volume of nonindustrial meltdown.

185. Stanley Publishing. *Directory of Mutual Savings Banks of United States.* New York, NY, 1924– . Annual.
Provides detailed financial analysis of assets, liabilities, deposits, and statements of condition of all mutual savings banks in the U.S.

186. ——. *National Factbook of Mutual Savings Banking.* New York, NY, 1958– . Annual.
Provides composite financial and operating data on the industry and contains performance measures.

187. Sunscape International. *Bank Acquisition Report.* Orlando, FL, 1980– . Monthly.
Contains detailed analyses of mergers and acquisitions among financial institutions, including the terms of mergers.

188. T.C.S. Capital Management. *CD Investors Guide of Key Financial Ratios of All FSLIC Insured Savings and Loans.* San Diego, CA, 1985– . Quarterly.
This fingertip statistical guide covers banks, savings and loans, trust departments, pension funds, credit unions, securities dealers, and investment advisors. Lists over 3,000 institutions alphabetically by state. Contains 14 primary financial indicators extracted from Federal Home Loan Bank reports.

189. T.K. Sanderson. *Directory of American Savings and Loan Associations.* Baltimore, MD, 1950– . Annual.
Provides comprehensive information on over 4,000 insured savings and loans as well as other thrifts.

190. Unidex. *Unidex Report.* Phoenix, AZ. Monthly.
Survey of consumer opinions on bank service. Includes topics like appeal of automatic bill payment, automatic transfer, variable rate mortgages, and automated teller machines, and a customer satisfaction index. Also given is information on sample size, age, income, occupation, and geographic locale of participants. In addition to the monthly surveys, *The Unidex Quarterly Reports* provide more extensive in-person interviewing conducted every 90 days. The *Marketlink* survey issued at varying frequency, provides the banker's point of view on specific bank services.

191. U.S. Agricultural Cooperative Service. *Top 100 Cooperatives: Financial Profile.* Washington, DC. Annual.
Report on finances and operations of the 100 largest cooperatives. Contains the number of cooperatives, revenues, and net worth, by cooperative type; debt capital, by source; aggregate balance sheets; net margins, by form of distribution; and net losses.

192. U.S. Board of Governors of the Federal Reserve System. *All-Bank Statistics, United States 1896–1955.* Washington, DC, 1959. 1229p.
Provides historical data on the number of banks and their principal assets, liabilities, and deposits by type.

193. ———. *Annual Report.* Washington, DC, 1914– . Annual.
This is a year-end summary of the nation's monetary and fiscal policies, major economic developments, and finances of member and nonmember banks. Includes the following data: monetary policy showing reserves, money supply, interest rates and international transactions; foreign currency operations; finances of the Federal Reserve banks, and statements of condition of other depository institutions.

194. ———. *Annual Statistical Digest.* Washington, DC, 1975– . Annual.
Presents data on the operations of the Federal Reserve banks, the banking industry in general, securities markets, federal finance, credit, and international finance. Tables include data on the money supply and reserves, interest rates, margin requirements, maximum interest rates payable on time and savings deposits, open market operations, deposits and deposit turnover at commercial banks, loans and investments at commercial banks, foreign exchange rates, and international transactions.

195. ———. *Banking and Monetary Statistics.* Washington, DC, 1943. 979p.
Data include historical time series in money market rates, commercial and finance company paper and banker's acceptances, bank rates on short-term business loans, and yields on government bonds. In most cases the data go back to 1890. Updated by a later edition, *Supplement to Banking and Monetary Statistics. Annual Statistical Digest* (1970–) keeps the information current.

196. ———. *Country Exposure Lending Survey.* Washington, DC. Semiannual.
The Comptroller of Currency, Federal Deposit Insurance Corporation, and Department of the Treasury conduct this semiannual survey. It

covers credits to foreign residents held at all domestic and foreign offices of more than 100 U.S. banking organizations. In addition to information on loans, loan maturities, types of borrowers, and loan guarantees, the survey also contains details on loan commitments to provide funds to foreigners. Statistical data are arranged by country.

197. ———. *Federal Reserve Bulletin.* Washington, DC. Monthly.
Reports on monetary and credit developments and related economic trends. In addition to articles, the monthly contains a detailed statistical appendix on monetary aggregates and reserves in depository institutions; interest rates; open market operations; loans, deposits, and debits in commercial banks; commercial assets and liabilities; commercial paper rates; prime interest rates; federal finance; consumer credit; flow of funds; government reserve assets; foreign banks' operations; claims on and by foreigners; discount rates of foreign central banks; foreign short-term interest rates; and foreign exchange rates.

198. ———. *Flow of Fund Accounts.* Washington, DC, 1975. 390p.
Provides data on the sources and uses of funds in the U.S. for the period 1945–1971. Since then, flow-of-funds statements have been published annually.

199. ———. *Flow of Funds: Accounts, Assets and Liabilities Outstanding.* Washington, DC. Annual.
Presents tables showing amounts of assets and liabilities outstanding at year-end for both the financial and nonfinancial sectors of the economy. Data are compiled to aid in analyzing the financial relationships among the various sectors and particularly for assessing the effects different monetary policies have on the general functioning of the economy. Flow-of-funds account data are also published monthly in the *Federal Reserve Bulletin* and quarterly in the *Federal Reserve Statistical Releases.* Includes data on credit market debt owed by nonfinancial and financial sectors with total outstanding for all sectors, by type; direct and indirect sources of funds to credit markets; sector statements of financial assets and liabilities; monetary and insurance reserves; gold and official foreign exchange holdings; Treasury currency and special drawing rights certificates; insurance and pension fund reserves; net interbank claims; currency and checkable deposits; time and savings deposits; money market mutual fund shares; federal funds and security repurchase agreements; U.S. deposits in foreign countries; U.S. Government securities; private securities; tax-exempt securities and loans; corporate and foreign bonds; corporate equities; consumer credit; and bank loans not elsewhere classified.

200. ———. *Functional Cost Analysis.* Washington, DC. Annual.
Provides details on income, expenses, and earnings for selected member banks in all 12 Federal Reserve districts. Data are used for measuring individual bank performance by peer groups. The aggregate statistics on average banks include income statements, balance sheets, and earnings by function grouped by banks with certain deposit size.

201. ———. *Historical Chart Book.* Washington, DC. Annual.
Historical chartbook showing U.S. financial and business trends from 1920. These data supplement current statistics contained in the quarterly *Federal Reserve Chart Book.* Contents include bank reserves and money

supply, reserves and related items of member banks, excess reserves and borrowings of member banks, monetary aggregates, money supply, income velocity of money, growth of monetary and banking aggregates, money supply components, thrift institution deposits, and demand deposit turnover. Also provides information on corporate security issues of nonfinancial corporation. Additional data cover consumer installment credit, financial assets held by households, household debt outstanding, mortgage installment credit, household borrowing, and mortgages and construction. Commercial banks are analyzed from the point of view of their assets and liabilities, loans and investments, and selected financial ratios. The stock and capital markets are also treated extensively.

202. ———. *Monthly Statistical Releases.* Washington, DC. Monthly.
Covers banking activity, consumer and business credit, interest rates, and bank stock transactions. Includes debits and deposit turnovers at commercial banks, consumer installment credit, finance companies, maturity distribution of outstanding negotiable time certificates of deposit at large commercial banks, selected interest rates, summary of equity security transactions, commercial and industrial loan commitments at selected large commercial banks, and assets and liabilities of international banking facilities.

203. ———. *Quarterly Statistical Releases.* Washington, DC. Quarterly.
Covers funds flow, farm finance, and foreign branches of U.S. banks. Includes flow-of-funds accounts, seasonally adjusted and unadjusted; geographical distribution of assets and liabilities of major foreign branches of U.S. banks; and agricultural finance data books consisting of farm credit conditions and lending operations.

204. ———. *Report on Priced Services.* Washington, DC. Quarterly.
Reports revenues and expenses for payment services provided to depository institutions by Federal Reserve banks. The services include commercial check collection, commercial automated clearing house services, wire transfer of funds, safe keeping, cash transportation by armored carrier, and coin wrapping.

205. ———. *Senior Loan Officer Opinion Survey of Bank Lending Practices.* Washington, DC. Irregular.
Covers the results of loan officer opinion surveys relating to anticipated business loan demand, consumer installment loan availability, business loan requirements, interest rates, mortgage loans, and sources and uses of funds.

206. ———. *Survey of Finance Companies.* Washington, DC. Quinquennial.
This survey is usually published as part of the *Federal Reserve Bulletin.* It is a very comprehensive report on the finance company industry, providing insight into the composition of finance company loan portfolios and their major sources of financing, including data on gross business and consumer receivables outstanding, number of finance companies and loans outstanding, finance company borrowing, and purchases of finance company commercial paper.

207. ———. *Weekly Statistical Releases.* Washington, DC. Weekly.
Covers various aspects of financial markets. Includes aggregate reserves of depository institutions and monetary base; assets and liabilities of domestically chartered and foreign related banking institutions; factors affecting reserves of depository institutions and statements of condition of Federal Reserve banks; money stock, liquid assets, and debit measures; selected borrowings in immediately available funds of large member banks; weekly consolidated reports of condition of large commercial banks and domestic subsidiaries; and selected interest and exchange rates.

208. U.S. Bureau of Government Financial Operations. *Report on Foreign Currencies Held by the U.S. Government.* Washington, DC. Semiannual.
Reports restricted and nonrestricted holdings of foreign currencies by the U.S. government. Data are shown in dollar equivalents computed at current exchange rates arranged by country. Includes an analysis of total foreign currencies held by government.

209. ———. *Statement of Foreign Currencies Purchased with Dollars.* Washington, DC. Semiannual.
Report on foreign currencies purchased by the U.S. government with dollars. Contains table showing value, by country, of each foreign currency purchased from outside sources for accommodation exchange and from the Treasury Department or commercial sources by the military and U.S. disbursing offices. Includes data on foreign currencies purchased by the U.S. with other foreign currencies.

210. U.S. Bureau of the Mint. *Annual Report of the Director of the Mint.* Washington, DC. Annual.
Contains detailed information on the operations of U.S. mints, assay offices, and bullion depositories. Includes data on the number and face value of U.S. coins manufactured, by mint; inventories of U.S. coins; shipments of newly manufactured U.S. coins for general circulation; medals and foreign coins manufactured by the U.S. Mint; and stocks and transactions of silver and gold.

211. ———. *Coinage Executed.* Washington, DC. Monthly.
Reports on the number and value of U.S. coins produced, by denomination, and the number of proof sets delivered by the San Francisco, Denver, and Philadelphia mints. Also contains data on the number of U.S. produced foreign coins, by country.

212. U.S. Comptroller of the Currency. *Annual Report.* Washington, DC. Annual.
The Comptroller of Currency is the regulatory authority over the national banking system. This publication reports the Comptroller's approval of new charters, mergers, and consolidation of banks as well as the financial condition of the national banking system.

213. ———. *Quarterly Journal.* Washington, DC. Quarterly.
Covers the activities of the national banking system in terms of financial condition, merger decisions, and enforcement actions of the Comptroller. Includes data on insolvent banks, bank consolidations, number of na-

tional banks, applications for new bank charters, and financial and operating data on national banks, including information on assets, liabilities, equity capital, net income, dividends, loan activity by type of loan, and operations of foreign branches.

214. ——. *Weekly Bulletin.* Washington, DC. Weekly.
Provides information on applications for new charters, approvals or denials, mergers, consolidations, and purchases of national banks. Also contains information on changes in the title as well as controlling ownerships of these banks.

215. U.S. Department of the Treasury. *Availability and Sale of Foreign Currencies to U.S. Tourists and Citizens.* Washington, DC. Semiannual.
Summary report containing amounts of excess foreign currencies held by the U.S. and sold to tourists and nonprofit organizations, arranged by country.

216. ——. *Foreign Currencies Held by U.S. Government.* Washington, DC. Semiannual.
Report on U.S. restricted and nonrestricted holdings of foreign currencies, shown in dollar equivalents at current exchange rates. Data arranged by country show value at each period.

217. ——. *Treasury Bulletin.* Washington, DC. Quarterly.
Originally issued as a monthly, this report includes current and historical data on capital movements between U.S. and foreign countries; sales and redemptions of U.S. Savings Bonds and Notes; distribution of federal securities, by class of investor and type of issue; estimated ownership of public debt securities, by private investors; Treasury market bid yields at constant maturities and yields on Treasury bill notes and bonds; average yields of long-term Treasury, corporate, and municipal bonds; U.S. reserve assets in terms of gold stock, foreign currencies, and special drawing rights; and liabilities to and claims on foreigners reported by banks in the U.S.

218. ——. *Treasury Reporting Rates of Exchange.* Washington, DC. Quarterly.
This is an official list, by country, of the amount of foreign currency accepted by U.S. disbursing offices in exchange for each dollar. Also contains substitute exchange rates for some countries.

219. U.S. Department of the Treasury, Savings Bonds Division. *Sales of U.S. Savings Bonds.* Washington, DC. Monthly.
Reports the sales of series EE and HH U.S. Savings Bonds, by state and territory. Includes information on redemptions, exchanges, and outstanding balances.

220. U.S. Federal Financial Institutions Examination Council. *Council Annual Report.* Washington, DC. Annual.
Report on FFIEC activities and finances. Tables show financial statements for the Council, U.S. commercial banks, and thrifts, by type of institution.

221. U.S. Government National Mortgage Association. *Annual Report.* Washington, DC. Annual.

Reports on the GNMA's purchases of mortgages under programs for selected types of housing for which usual financing is not available, management and liquidation of certain federally owned mortgages, and the mortgage-backed securities program to channel new funds into residential financing. Contents include mortgage commitments, purchases, statements of financial condition, operations, retained earnings, changes in financial position, and a summary of financial statistics.

222. U.S. League of Savings Institutions. *Savings and Loan Fact Book.* Chicago, IL, 1954– . Annual.

Provides composite financial and operating data on the savings and loan industry. Includes data on mortgage interest rates and residential finance.

223. ———. *Savings and Mortgage Lending Trends.* Chicago, IL. Monthly.

Contains information on savings and loan activity in terms of the flow of funds, loan commitments, and advances.

224. ———. *Savings Institutions Sourcebook.* Chicago, IL, 1984– . Annual.

Presents detailed information on savings institutions' lending activities and financial conditions, trends, and selected comparisons to other types of financial institutions. Included in the annual publication are composite data on savings, mortgage lendings, and other activities of savings institutions and federal agencies. Statistics include the allocation of household funds, annual change in financial assets of households, average yields on selected investments, total volume of savings at savings institutions, the flow of savings, growth in selected types of credit, mortgage loans outstanding, long-term interest rates, yields on corporate issues, effective home mortgage interest rates, terms on conventional mortgage loans, and mortgage portfolio activity.

225. Veribanc Inc. *Veribanc Reports.* Woburn, MA, 1981– . Frequency varies.

This data-processing firm was established in 1981 to provide individuals and businesses access to more financial information about their banks, savings and loans, and credit unions. The company publishes several reports designed to meet specific needs. *Bank or Savings and Loan Research Report*, a compilation of the statement of condition and income data, is available for individual institutions. *Short Form Report*, giving a brief overview of the financial condition of all commercial banks, mutual savings institutions, and savings and loan credit unions, is available for individual institutions. *Bank Holding Company Research Report* is a compilation of statements of condition and income data based on a consolidation of figures from holding companies. *Holding Company Short Form Report*, available for individual holding companies, provides a brief overview of member banks' consolidated accounts. A compilation of data for each of the member banks as well as a summary in consolidated form is available in the *Holding Company Member Reports*. The *Blue Bank Report* provides a list of commercial banks, arranged by geographical region, meeting a very high standard in profitability, equity-to-assets ratio, liquidity, and size. *The City Five or County Five Report* provides a list of the five highest ranking commercial banks or savings and loans meeting the same criteria as above. *The Loan Acceleration Report* provides information on repayment schedules.

Veribanc also publishes reports identifying all federally insured institutions which fall under a particular category. These reports are based on the latest information available to the regulatory agencies. The categories include banks and savings and loans which could reach zero equity or net worth within one year, institutions operating with equity or net worth of a specified percentage of their assets, institutions with liquid assets less than a specified percentage of their deposits, and banks with liabilities greater than twice their liquid assets. Other criteria include excess foreign loans, substandard loans, profitability ratios, problem loans, loan reserves, and property holdings. All the foregoing data are available in hard copy and on diskettes. A special series, *Foreign Lending Exposure Reports*, provides totals by country of aggregate indebtedness to all U.S. banks; amounts of short-term and long-term debts owed to specific banks, arranged by country; and lists of U.S. banks that are lenders to foreign countries, which are specified.

226. Warren, Gorham & Lamont. *Banker's Diary and Guide*. Boston, MA. Annual.

This leading desk reference of the banking community contains banking information such as the following: money-market investments, all-savers account regulations, annual percentage rates on discount rate loans, bad check laws, bank holidays, certificates of deposit, collateral loans, commercial paper, interest rate tables, tax schedules, and a description of state and federal agencies dealing with bankruptcy.

227. ———. *Depository Institutions Performance Directory*. Boston, MA, 1986– . Annual.

Published in two volumes, Volume 1 covers commercial banks and Volume 2 savings and loans and thrifts. Provides data for the evaluation of the financial condition and performance of all depository institutions. Quarterly as well as annual data are available on the size and growth of the institutions, loan and investment portfolios, market valuation, deposit size, net worth, income performance, and asset quality. Rankings are presented by state, deposit size groupings, and regional peer groupings. Quarterly updates are included in the annual subscription.

Foreign Country Sources

AFGHANISTAN

228. Bank of Afghanistan. *Afghan Financial Statistics.* Kabul, Afghanistan, 1964– . Irregular.

Contains financial statistics such as foreign assets, public debt, bank deposits, money, and capital. Data on money supply, foreign exchange, and interest rates are also available from the bank's *Quarterly Bulletin.* Because of the political situation in the country, national data sources on money and banking are hard to come by. Researchers have therefore to depend on external sources such as *Country Reports,* formerly known as *Quarterly Economic Reviews,* from the Economic Intelligence Unit (London).

ANGOLA

229. Banco de Angola. *Economic and Financial Survey of Angola.* Lisbon, Portugal, 1960–1973.

Until it ceased publication in 1973, this annual report contained data on the monetary situation in Angola. So did the *Boletim trimestral,* which was last issued in the *Anuário estatístico* from the Instituto nacional de estadistico in Angola.

ANTIGUA

230. East Caribbean Common Market. Secretariat. *Annual Digest of Statistics.* St. Johns, Antigua. Annual.

Covers the islands of Anguilla, St. Kitts, Nevis, Montserrat, Dominica, St. Lucia, St. Vincent, Grenada, and Grenadines. Provides statistics on banking and interest rates.

AUSTRALIA

231. Reserve Bank of Australia. *Statistical Bulletin.* Sydney, Australia, 1960– . Monthly.

This is a supplement to the *Annual Report.* It contains data on banking, money supply, interest rates, and capital and credit markets. The Australian Bureau of Statistics also publishes a quarterly, *Banking,* covering the nation's trading and savings banks, interest rates, and money supply. The annual cumulation of the same is *Banking, Insurance and Other Private Finance*. A monthly and annual report, *Finance Companies*, includes composite banking and financial data. A similar monthly report, *Finance Corporation Statistics*, covers building societies and credit cooperatives. The various state financial institutions are covered in the annual *Private Finance*. The *Treasury Information Bulletin* from the Australian Government Publishing Service also deals with banking and finance.

AUSTRIA

232. Österreichische Nationalbank. *Annual Report.* Vienna, Austria. Annual.

Provides detailed statistics on money, credit, and the capital market. Another monthly, *Austria's Monetary Situation*, abridged from the *Mitteilungen* contains monetary statistics. A directory of Austrian banks and other credit institutions is the annual *Finanz-Compass Österreich* published by the Compass Verlag.

BAHAMAS

233. Central Bank of the Bahamas. *Quarterly Review.* Nassau, Bahamas, 1974– . Quarterly.

Contains data on the monetary situation in the country. More extensive data are available from the Department of Statistics' *Quarterly Statistical Summary* and annual *Statistical Abstract*. They include information on treasury bills, money supply, commercial banks, interest rates, and financial institutions.

BAHRAIN

234. Bahrain Monetary Agency. *Annual Report.* Manama, Bahrain. Annual.

Covers the monetary policies of the agency for the year. The agency's *Quarterly Statistical Bulletin* provides statistics on money and banking. So does the Statistical Bureau's annual *Statistical Abstract*.

BANGLADESH

235. Bangladesh Bank. *Annual Report.* Dhaka, Bangladesh, 1974– . Annual.

In addition to covering the bank's monetary policies, the report contains a general summary of the financial situation in the country. Monetary statistics are also available from the bank's other publications, such as the monthly *Bangladesh Bank Bulletin* and the quarterly *Scheduled Banks Statistics* covering private commercial banks. The Ministry of Finance's annual *Economic Survey* and the Bureau of Statistics' *Monthly Statistical Bulletin* also contain composite data on the monetary situation.

BARBADOS

236. Central Bank of Barbados. *Annual Statistical Digest.* Bridgetown, Barbados, 1976– . Annual.
Data cover the central bank and commercial banks. Includes information on money supply and interest and exchange rates. Data are supplemented by the *Quarterly Report* and *Monthly Economic and Financial Statistics.* Similar statistics are available from the Barbados Statistical Services' annual *Financial Statistics.*

BELGIUM

237. Banque nationale de Belgique. *Bulletin de la banque nationale de Belgique.* Brussels, Belgium, 1971– . Monthly.
Reports on developments in banking and the activities of the financial institutions in the country. Statistics include foreign exchange rates, credit and capital markets, and interest rates. Detailed survey of the country's banking is available from *Rapports annuels* and *Statistiques économiques belges.* The Caisse generale d' épargne et de retraite publishes related financial information in the *Rapport Annuel* and *Bulletin économique et financier.* Two other institutions publishing financial information are the Commission bancaire and Credit communal de Belgique.

BELIZE

238. Belize. Central Planning Unit. *Annual Abstract of Statistics.* Belmopan, Belize. Annual.
Reports on the accounts of government savings bank, currency in circulation, commercial banks, and credit unions.

BENIN

239. Benin. Ministère du Plan et de la prospective. *Annuaire statistique.* Cotonou, Benin, 1973– . Annual.
Analysis of the monetary sector includes data on money, credit, and balance of payments.

BOLIVIA

240. Banco central de Bolivia. *Boletín estadístico.* La Paz, Bolivia. Quarterly.
Covers the country's monetary and fiscal policies, including money supply, interest and exchange rates, and credit. The bank's annual report (1929–), *Memoria anual,* contains similar information. A bimonthly, *Suplemento estadístico,* provides information on money supply, gold reserves, and composite statistics on Bolivian banks and exchange rates.

BOTSWANA

241. Bank of Botswana. *Annual Report.* Gaborone, Botswana, 1976– . Annual.
> Reports on the activities of the central bank. The statistical appendix contains data on the nation's banking and finance. Similar information is available from the Central Statistical Office's annual *Statistical Abstract* and its monthly supplement, *Statistical Bulletin.*

BRAZIL

242. Banco central do Brasil. *Boletim.* Rio de Janeiro, Brazil, 1967– . Monthly.
> Provides detailed statistics on the banking and financial systems. The bank's *Relatório annual* and *Boletim trimestral* as well as the Ministerio da fazenda's monthly *Estatísticas tributárias básicas* provide similar information.

BURUNDI

243. Banque de la République du Burundi. *Rapport annuel.* Bujumbura, Burundi, 1970– . Annual.
> Reports on the bank's activities as well as on the banking and monetary developments in the country. Covers currency, money supply, and foreign exchange. Additional information is available from the *Bulletin mensuel, Bulletin trimestriel,* and *Note sur le credit au secteur prive.*

CANADA

244. Bank of Canada. *Annual Report of the Governor to the Minister of Finance and Statement of Accounts.* Ottawa, Canada, 1955– . Annual.
> Covers the bank's activities in monetary policy. The monthly *Review* provides banking and other financial statistics. The information is updated by the bank's *Weekly Financial Statistics.* Selected banking data are available from the Canadian Bankers Association's bimonthly *Canadian Banker.* In addition, Statistics Canada, a government agency, publishes reports such as *Credit Unions, Consumer Credit, Checks Cashed, Financial Flow Accounts, Financial Capital Flows and Stocks, Survey of Consumer Finance,* and *Financial Institutions' Financial Statistics.*

245. BCA Publications. *Bank Credit Analyst.* Montreal, Canada, 1949– . Monthly.
> Contains statistical data and analysis of trends in the Canadian financial market.

246. CCH Canadian. *Canadian Financial Institutions.* Don Mills, Ontario, Canada, 1983– . Monthly.
> Contains summary description, including financial information, on banks in Canada.

247. Canadian Bankers Association. *Bank Facts: Chartered Banks of Canada.* Toronto, Canada, 1968– . Annual.
   Formerly entitled *Factbook: Chartered Banks of Canada,* this publication provides composite financial data on Canadian chartered banks.

248. Canadian Daily Quotation Service Ltd. *Canadian Financial E-Z Directory.* Toronto, Canada, 1964– . Annual.
   Provides financial and related information on Canadian banks, trust companies, and other financial institutions.

249. Canadian Payments Association. *Banking Directory of Canada.* Toronto, Canada, 1980– . Annual with bimonthly supplements.
   Contains statistical and related information on major banking institutions in the country.

250. Trust Companies Association of Canada. *Directory of Canadian Trust Companies.* Toronto, Canada, 1953– . Annual.
   Provides summary financial and related information on Canadian banking trusts.

CHILE

251. Banco central de Chile. *Annual Report Presented to the Banking Superintendent.* Santiago, Chile, 1927– . Annual.
   Reviews the banking operations in the preceding year. For statistical data it would be more advisable to use the Bank's monthly *Boletín mensual* (1928–) containing tables on money and banking. Similar information is available from the Superintendencia de Bancòs monthly *Boletín estadístico* covering the banking sector.

CHINA (Republic of China)

252. Central Bank of China. *Taiwan Financial Statistics Monthly.* Taipei, Taiwan, 1962–1978. 35 vols.
   Contains banking, financial, and foreign exchange data.

COLOMBIA

253. Banco de la República (Colombia). *Revista del banco de la república.* Bogotá, Colombia, 1927– . Monthly.
   Reviews the current situation and developments in banks and financial institutions. Comparable data are also available from the annual *Anuario de fiscales y financieras,* issued by the Departamento administrativo nacional de estadística.

COSTA RICA

254. Banco central de Costa Rica. *Boletín estadístico mensual.* San Jose, Costa Rica, 1950– . Monthly.
   This is a monthly statistical bulletin containing data on money, banking, and credit and capital markets. Another monthly, *Crédito y cuentas monetarias,* reviews the credit and monetary situation in the country.

CYPRUS

255. Central Bank of Cyprus. *Annual Report of the Board of Directors.* Nicosia, Cyprus, 1963/64– . Annual.
    This is a general overview of the country's banking, credit, and monetary situation as well as finanicial outlook. The bimonthly *Bulletin* (1960–) provides data on money, banking, interest rates, yields, and foreign exchange. Banking and currency developments are also covered in the Ministry of Finance's annual *Statistics Abstract* and *Quarterly Statistical Digest.*

DENMARK

256. Danmarks nationalbank. *Arsberetning.* Copenhagen, Denmark. Annual.
    This report of the central bank contains commentary on monetary policy and includes data on foreign exchange, credit, finance, and the money market. The quarterly *Monetary Review* (1967–) covers commercial banks, money supply, interest rates, and mortgage markets. Data on international liquidity, foreign exchange, and commercial and savings banks are also available from the *statistiske efetrretninger* and *Konjunkturoversigt,* published by Danmarks statistik, and the *Annual Report* published by Tilsynet med banker og sparekasser, the country's bank supervision board.

DOMINICAN REPUBLIC

257. Banco central de la República Dominicana. *Boletín mensual.* Santo Domingo, Dominican Republic, 1948– . Monthly.
    Also sometimes entitled *Cuadros estadísticos,* this bulletin contains statistics on the country's banks, monetary situation, capital movements, and foreign exchange. Similar data are available from the monthly *Estados financieras.* The country's statistical service, Oficina nacional de estadística, publishes an annual, *Estadística bancaria,* covering the banking and monetary sectors of the national economy.

ECUADOR

258. Banco central del Ecuador. *Memoria del Gerente General del Banco central del Ecuador.* Quito, Ecuador, 1975– . Annual.
    Covers the country's monetary policy, credit and capital markets, foreign exchange, and external debt. Similar data are also available from the annual *Boletín* (1978–) and the occasional report *Información estadística.* Data on money supply and banking activity are also provided by the *Boletín de estadísticas,* issued semiannually by the Ministerio de finanzas.

EGYPT

259. Al-Bank al-Markazi al-Misri. Central Bank of Egypt. *Report of the Board of Directors.* Cairo, Egypt, 1974– . Annual.
   Surveys national and international monetary trends, banking, and foreign exchange. A quarterly *Review* covers similar topics.

EL SALVADOR

260. Banco central de reserva de El Salvador. *Revista mensual.* San Salvador, El Salvador, 1934– . Monthly.
   Contains data on international reserves, money supply, credit, and banking. The quarterly *Revista trimestral* and annual *Memoria* contain additional banking and financial information.

FINLAND

261. Suomen pankki. Bank of Finland. *Vuosikirja (Yearbook).* Helsinki, Finland, 1914/20– . Annual.
   Provides such financial and banking statistics as interest and exchange rates, foreign exchange reserves, bank deposits and loans, and other money and capital market indicators. The bank also publishes a *Monthly Bulletin* (1918–) which provides similar and updated statistics. Another monthly bulletin, published in Finnish, *Valutastallningen,* surveys the foreign exchange situation.

FRANCE

262. Banque de France. *Compte rendu: Banque de France.* Paris, France, 1973– . Annual.
   Statistical data cover financial developments, money, and credit. Supplemented by the *Bulletin trimestriel* (1971–). The Société Generale publishes a monthly analysis entitled *Situation financière,* as well as an annual called *Bilans des banques.* The Conseil national du credit publishes data on the monetary situation in the annual *Le Monnaie,* in the quarterly report entitled *Bulletin trimestriel* surveying developments in the credit market, in a *Rapport annuel,* and in the *Statistiques mensuelles.*

GAMBIA

263. Central Bank of the Gambia. *Quarterly Bulletin.* Banjul, Gambia, 1971– . Quarterly.
   Includes data on money, banking, and public finance.

GHANA

264. Bank of Ghana. *Report of the Board of Directors.* Accra, Ghana, 1957– . Annual.
   Reviews developments and statistical information on financial, fiscal, and monetary policies of the country. Supplemented by the *Quarterly*

Economic Bulletin (1960–), which deals with banking activities, interest rates, and money supply.

GUATEMALA

265. Banco de Guatemala. *Estudio económico y memoria de labores.* Guatemala City, Guatemala, 1945– . Annual.
Reviews the economic and financial conditions in the country with special reference to monetary and banking situations and developments. More up-to-date and detailed data on Guatemalan banking and money are available from the monthly *Balance mensual* and quarterly *Boletín estadístico* (both 1945–). The Superintendencia de bancos publishes an annual *Boletín de estadísticas bancarias* which contains detailed data on the nation's commercial banks and trust companies.

GUYANA

266. Bank of Guyana. *Annual Report.* Georgetown, Guyana. Annual.
Reviews the operation of the central bank in the areas of currency, foreign exchange, and monetary policy. Data are supplemented by the monthly *Economic Bulletin* dealing with the credit and capital markets, treasury operations, and investments. The *Monthly Statistical Bulletin* also contains financial statistics.

HONDURAS

267. Banco central de Honduras. *Memoria: Banco central de Honduras.* Tegucigalpa, Honduras, 1950– . Annual.
Covers, among other things, banking structure, monetary situation, credit market, and public finance. The monthly *Boletín estadístico,* (1951–) contains current information in these areas. The activities of the central bank itself are reported in the monthly *Balance.*

HONG KONG

268. Hong Kong. Census and Statistics Dept. *Monthly Digest of Statistics.* Hong Kong. Monthly.
Money, banking, and finance is a major portion of this monthly report on basic conditions in Hong Kong.

HUNGARY

269. Magyar nemzeti bank. National Bank of Hungary. *Quarterly Review.* Budapest, Hungary, 1983– . Quarterly.
Also called the *Economic Bulletin of the National Bank of Hungary,* this periodical provides comprehensive data on the country's banking activities.

Foreign Country Sources 51

ICELAND

270. Sedlabanki Islands. Central Bank of Iceland. *Annual Report.* Reykjavík, Iceland, 1961– . Annual.
Provides comprehensive data on money and credit markets and foreign exchange. A triennial, *Fjarmalatioinde (Financial Review),* provides similar commentary on the banking situation.

INDIA

271. Reserve Bank of India. *Report on Currency and Finance.* Bombay, India, 1935/36– . Annual.
As is evident from the title, this periodical deals with currency and banking developments in the country. Data on financial flows, money supply, interest rates, credit markets, and foreign exchange are available in the *Annual Report on the Working of the Reserve Bank and Trend and Progress of Banking in India* (1949–). A statistical summary of banking and finance is also available in the monthly *Bulletin* (1947–).

INDONESIA

272. Bank Indonesia. *Report of the Governor.* Djakarta, Indonesia, 1953– . Annual.
Annual commentary on the national banking and financial situation. It is supplemented by a *Monthly Bulletin* and *Weekly Report* dealing with money supply, interest rates, foreign exchange, and banking. The Bureau of Statistics publishes similar data in its annual *Stistik kenangen (Financial Statistics).*

IRAQ

273. Al-Bank al-markazi al-Íraqi. *Annual Report.* Baghdad, Iraq, 1949– . Annual.
A review of the activities of the central bank relating to monetary policy, situation, and outlook. Supplemented by the quarterly *Bulletin,* which provides detailed financial statistics on banking, currency, and foreign exchange.

IRELAND

274. Central Bank of Ireland. *Annual Report.* Dublin, Ireland. Annual.
Contains information on the country's monetary policy and other financial data. Supplemented by the quarterly *Faisnésis ráithiúil.*

ISRAEL

275. Bank Yisrael (Bank of Israel). *Annual Report.* Jerusalem, Israel, 1975– . Annual.
This is the annual report of the central bank to the Knesset reviewing the economic and monetary situations and outlook. The bank also publishes a monthly *Seker (Economic Review)* covering finances.

ITALY

276. Banca d'Italia. *Abridged Version of the Report for the Year . . . , Presented by the Governor to the Ordinary General Meeting of Shareholders.* Rome, Italy. Annual.
Contains statistical tables covering money and financial markets, exchange rates, and monetary activities of the bank. A more comprehensive version of this is *Relazione annuale considerazione finale appendice.* The *Bolletino,* published quarterly, and *Supplemento al Bolletino* update the annual edition. Individual Italian banks also publish financial information.

277. Euromoney Publications. *Italian Credit Structures.* London, England, 1986. 288p.
Written by the Bank of Italy, this publication provides a unique and invaluable insight into the workings of the Italian banking and credit system.

JAMAICA

278. Bank of Jamaica. *Report and Statement of Accounts.* Kingston, Jamaica, 1961– . Annual.
Reviews monetary developments, credit and capital markets, currency, banking, and foreign exchange. Similar data are available from the *Monthly Review* and *Quarterly Bulletin.* The Department of Statistics publishes an annual *Statistical Abstract,* which includes information on commercial banks, interest rates, treasury bills, credit unions, and trusts. Major financial units of Jamaica are covered by the Department's annual *Monetary Statistics.*

JAPAN

279. Bank of Japan. *Economic Statistics Annual.* Tokyo, Japan. Annual.
In combination with its supplement, *Economic Statistics Monthly,* this publication gives detailed statistics on money and banking, reserve rates, discount markets, consumer credit, interest rates, accounts of city and regional banks, savings institutions, credit associations and other financial institutions, government security yields, and foreign exchange rates. The Industrial Bank of Japan publishes the *IBJ Monthly Report* covering the short-term money market, money supply, and financial institutions. The Bureau of Statistics also issues reports such as the *Monthly Statistics of Japan* containing banking and financial data.

280. Euromoney Publications. *Japanese Finance.* London, England, 1985. 217p.
Contains a thorough analysis of Japan's financial institutions and markets. Includes details on long-term credit; trust and foreign banks; securities houses; finance and trading companies; role of the Bank of Japan; and data on Japanese stock, bond, money, and foreign exchange markets.

281. Japan. Ministry of Finance. *Financial Statistics of Japan.* Tokyo, Japan. 1952– . Annual.
    Formerly entitled *Bulletin of Financial Statistics,* this publication, issued by the Institute of Fiscal and Monetary Policy, provides statistical information on the commercial banking industry in Japan.

JORDAN

282. Central Bank of Jordan. *Annual Report.* Amman, Jordan. Annual.
    Reviews financial and monetary developments. The *Monthly Statistical Bulletin* contains data on money, banking, exchange rates, foreign exchange permits, money supply, and currency. The Department of Statistics' *Statistical Yearbook* also contains data on banking, currency, and foreign exchange.

KAMPUCHEA

283. Banque nationale du Cambodge. *Bulletin mensuel.* Phnom Penh, Kampuchea (Cambodia), 1955– . Monthly.
    Contains statistics on money and credit markets. However, since the revolution data on this country are not easy to come by.

KENYA

284. Central Bank of Kenya. *Annual Report: Central Bank of Kenya.* Nairobi, Kenya, 1966– . Annual.
    Survey of financial and monetary situation including financial institutions. The quarterly *Economic and Financial Review* covers the foreign exchange situation, including exchange rates, commercial banks, money supply, and general interest rates. The Central Bureau of Statistics also publishes an annual *Economic Survey* covering money, banking, foreign exchange rates, interest rates, reserves, money supply, liquidity, and government finances as well as a monthly *Statistics of Commercial Banks.*

LEBANON

285. Banque du Liban (Bank of Lebanon). *Rapport.* Beirut, Lebanon. Annual.
    Reviews the financial and banking system in the country which used to be known as the Switzerland of the Middle East. Data containing information on money and banking is also available from the Direction centrale de la statistique's *Bulletin mensuel.*

LIBERIA

286. National Bank of Liberia. *Annual Report.* Monrovia, Liberia, 1974– . Annual.
    Reports on the monetary activities of the bank, including data on banking and public finance. The monthly *Statistical Bulletin* contains similar

but updated information. The Ministry of Planning published *Quarterly Statistics Bulletin,* which has become an annual in recent years, dealing with the commercial banking industry.

LIBYA

287. Central Bank of Libya. *Annual Report.* Tripoli, Libya. 1955– . Annual.

Commentary on gold market, interest rates, money, banking developments, currency, and foreign exchange. The monthly *Economic Bulletin* (1966–) contains data on commercial banks, money supply, and foreign exchange, as does the Department of Census and Statistics' annual *Statistical Abstract.*

LUXEMBOURG

288. Luxembourg. Caisse d'épargne de l'etat du Grand-Duche de Luxembourg. Banque de l'etat. *Rapport et bilans.* Luxembourg City, Luxembourg.

Covers the credit markets and interest rates. Money supply and currency information is available from the *Bulletin trimestriel* published by the Commissariat au contrôle des banques.

MALAWI

289. Reserve Bank of Malawi. *Report on Accounts: Reserve Bank of Malawi.* Blantyre, Malawi. Annual.

Annual report of the bank's activities and financial developments. The quarterly *Financial and Economic Review* (1972–) contains data on the financial sector, monetary system, commercial banks, and foreign exchange.

MALAYSIA

290. Bank Negera. Malaysia. *Annual Report.* Kuala Lumpur, Malaysia, 1980– . Annual.

In addition to a statement of accounts, this report contains commentary on the monetary and financial developments in the country. The *Quarterly Economic Bulletin* (1968–) and the *Monthly Statistical Supplement* contain updated banking and financial information.

MALTA

291. Central Bank of Malta. *Annual Report and Statement of Accounts: Central Bank of Malta.* Valletta, Malta, 1968– . Annual.

Report on the activities of the central bank including data on money, finance, commercial banking, capital markets, interest rates, and foreign exchange. The data are updated by the *Quarterly Review* (1967–).

MAURITIUS

292. Bank of Mauritius. *Annual Report.* Port Louis, Mauritius. Annual.
Reports on the central bank's monetary policies. Also provides information on commercial banks, money supply, and currency. Developments in the financial markets are covered by the *Quarterly Review.*

MEXICO

293. Banamex. Banco nacional de Mexico. *Review of the Economic Situation of Mexico.* Mexico City, Mexico, 1924– . Monthly.
Contains information on money supply, exchange rates, interest rates, treasury certificate rates, promissory note rates, and current balances at the Banco nacional de Mexico. The *Annual Report* (1925–) and the monthly *Indicadores económicos* contain additional information on money supply, money and capital markets, and foreign exchange. The Comision nacional bancaria y de seguros publishes a monthly *Boletín estadístico* containing statistics on banking and savings institutions.

MOROCCO

294. Bank al-Maghrib. Banque du Maroc. *Rapport.* Rabat, Morocco. Annual.
Reviews the economic and monetary situation, including data on banking, finance, and investments. The quarterly *Etudes et statistiques* covers movements in interest and exchange rates.

NEPAL

295. Nepal Rastra Bank. *Annual Report on Operations and Accounts.* Kathmandu, Nepal. Annual.
Covers the activities of the central bank. Its *Quarterly Bulletin* (1966–) provides statistical information on money, banking and credit, treasury operations, government securities, and the foreign exchange situation.

NETHERLANDS

296. Nederlandsche bank. *Report.* Amsterdam, The Netherlands, 1945– . Annual.
Provides a general review of monetary and financial developments, money and capital markets, banking and giro institutions, and international money and foreign exchange markets. *Quarterly Statistics* provides data on financial institutions, money supply, interest rates, and foreign currency exchange markets.

NEW ZEALAND

297. Reserve Bank of New Zealand. *Annual Report of the Directors and Statement of Accounts.* Wellington, New Zealand. Annual.
   Surveys the financial performance of trading banks, savings banks, finance companies, and building societies and reports on the money and mortgage markets and foreign exchange. The *Monthly Bulletin* (1937–) supplements the *Annual Report.*

NICARAGUA

298. Banco central de Nicaragua. *Informe anual.* Managua, Nicaragua, 1961– . Annual.
   Reports on the central bank's monetary and credit policies. Also provides an analysis of the financial system in the country. Data on money, banking, and foreign exchange are available from the semiannual *Boletín semestral.*

NIGERIA

299. Central Bank of Nigeria. *Annual Report and Statement of Accounts.* Lagos, Nigeria, 1959– . Annual.
   Reviews monetary policies and the financial system. The biannual *Developments in the Nigerian Economy* (1971–) also covers banking. Another biannual report, *Economic and Financial Review* (1963–), provides information on commercial banks, money supply, and capital markets. A statistical summary of commercial banking activities is available from the monthly *Commercial Bank Activities.* The *Monthly Report* (1969–) deals with flow of funds and foreign exchange developments.

NORWAY

300. Norges bank. *Economic Bulletin.* Oslo, Norway, 1929– . Quarterly.
   Every issue contains a statistical section covering banking and financial statistics such as credit markets, foreign exchange, and currency. The *Annual Report* provides commentaries on credit and foreign exchange markets. The Statistisk sentralbyra is also a good source for data on banking and finance. They publish reports such as the annual *Kredittmarbedstatistikk* on credit markets. Private sources of similar information include publications from A.S. Okonomisk Literatur such as the annual *Savings Banks in Norway* and *Commercial Banks in Norway.*

PAKISTAN

301. Sanaullah Publications. *Pakistan Banking Directory.* Karachi, Pakistan, 1966– . Annual.
   Provides comprehensive financial data on commercial banks in Pakistan.

302. State Bank of Pakistan. *Bulletin.* Karachi, Pakistan, 1951– .
Supplements *Banking Statistics of Pakistan* (1975), which provides comprehensive data on the country's banking industry, including state banks, scheduled banks, cooperative banks, clearing houses, and credit markets.

PARAGUAY

303. Banco central del Paraguay. Departamento de estudios económicos. *Reseña económica financiera y monetaria.* Asunción, Paraguay, 1954– . Annual.
Reviews the financial situation in the country including data on money supply, credit market, international reserves, and foreign exchange. A monthly *Boletín estadístico* also covers the monetary situation.

PERU

304. Banco central de reserva del Peru. *Boletín.* Lima, Peru, 1931– . Monthly.
Contains not only financial, banking, and monetary data on the whole country but also information on the following banks: Banco agrario, Banco industrial, Banco minero, Banco de la vivienda, and Banco central ilipotecario. Similar information is available from the annual *Memoria* (1937–). The Superintendencia de Banca y Seguros publishes *Boletín estadístico bancario,* which provides quarterly summaries of banking statistics.

PHILIPPINES

305. Central Bank of the Philippines. *Annual Report.* Manila, Philippines, 1949– . Annual.
Reviews the central bank's monetary policies. Includes statistics such as money, credit and financial markets, and foreign exchange policy and rates. The appendix, subtitled *Statistical Bulletin,* provides data on money and banking, money supply, international reserves, foreign exchange, domestic credit, savings banks, rural banks, and nonfinancial banking institutions. The quarterly *The Philippine Financial Statistics* (1970–) covers similar topics plus interest rates and yields, the money market, and financial institutions. The financial system of the country is described in the annual *Fact Book of the Philippine Financial System* (1976–). News of financial and monetary trends is available from the weekly *CB Review* (1928–).

RWANDA

306. Banque nationale du Rwanda. *Bulletin.* Kigali, Rwanda, 1981– . Quarterly.
Reports on the activities of the central bank and gives some monetary statistics.

SAUDI ARABIA

307. Falcon Publishing. *Arab Banking and Finance Handbook.* Manama, Bahrain, 1983– . Annual.
   Provides statistical data on the financial institutions doing business in Saudi Arabia, Jordan, Egypt, and Kuwait.

308. Múassasat al-Naqd al-Árabi al-Saaudi. Sáudi Arabian Monetary Agency. Research and Statistics Department. *Annual Report.* Riyadh, Saudi Arabia, 1960– . Annual.
   Reviews monetary trends, banking, and currency. Similar information is also available from the irregular *Statistical Summary.*

SIERRA LEONE

309. Bank of Sierra Leone. *Quarterly Statistical Review.* Freetown, Sierra Leone, 1965– . Quarterly.
   Also called *Economic Review,* this report covers the national financial situation with time series statistical data on central banking, money supply, and commercial banks. The bank's monetary policies can be obtained from its *Report and Annual Statement of Accounts,* (1974–).

SINGAPORE

310. Consulton Ltd. *Banks and Financial Institutions in Singapore: The Consulton Report.* Singapore, 1976– . Annual.
   Provides a directory and statistical information on the banking institutions in the country.

311. Monetary Authority of Singapore. *Directory of Financial Institutions.* Singapore. Annual.
   Provides data on the nation's commercial banks, merchant banks, discount houses, finance companies, and international money brokers. The Monetary Authority's *Annual Report* gives additional information on monetary trends, exchange rates, the capital market, and nonbank financial institutions.

SOMALIA

312. Central Bank of Somalia. *Annual Report and Statement of Accounts.* Mogadishu, Somalia. Annual.
   Covers the nation's banking system, including the activities of the Somali national banks. Includes a survey of monetary activities. The quarterly *Bulletin* provides updated information on the above topics.

SOUTH AFRICA

313. South African Reserve Bank. *Annual Economic Report.* Pretoria, South Africa. Annual.
   Together with *Monthly Money and Banking Statistics* and *Quarterly Bulletin,* this annual provides information on the country's monetary sector. Similar information is available from the Department of Statis-

tics' biennial *South African Statistics,* which provides composite data on banking and finance.

SOUTH KOREA

314. Hanguk Unhaeng. Bank of Korea. *Annual Report.* Seoul, Korea, 1950– . Annual.

Analyzes monetary, credit, and foreign exchange policies during the year. The bank also has been publishing a quarterly, *Foreign Exchange Statistics,* detailing the foreign exchange situation and rates, and *Monthly Economic Indicators,* containing data on financial institutions. The National Bureau of Statistics publishes an annual *Statistical Handbook,* an abridged version of *Statistical Yearbook* containing data on banking and finance. The Economic Planning Board publishes *Monthly Statistics of Korea,* covering, among other things, money, currency, and foreign exchange rates.

SPAIN

315. Banco de España. *Boletín estadístico.* Madrid, Spain, 1960– . Monthly.

Provides detailed statistics on the central bank, commercial banks, credit and securities markets, and interest rates. Historical data on the same subjects are available from the irregular *Boletín estadístico: Series historicas.* The banking sector is also partially covered by the monthly *Boletín económico* and *Informe anual.*

SRI LANKA

316. Sri Lanka, Maha Bankuva. Central Bank of Ceylon. *Staff Studies.* Colombo, Sri Lanka, 1971– . Semiannual.

Contains textual and statistical reviews of the country's banking sector and money rates. The annual *Report of the Monetary Board to the Minister of Finance* (1951–) covers the entire economy, including the financial sector. The monthly *Bulletin* (1951–) provides current information on money and banking, savings and credit markets, and foreign exchange. Banking and finance companies are also treated in the annual economic review, *Arthika vivaranya* (1975–), which deals with the country's economic situation.

SUDAN

317. Bank al-Sudan. *Annual Report.* Khartoum, Sudan, 1959– . Annual.

Provides data on money supply, currency, foreign exchange, banking, and credit. Supplemented by quarterly *Economic and Financial Statistics Review* (1959–), which includes information on commercial banks.

SURINAME

318. Centrale bank van Suriname. *Verslag.* Paramaribo, Suriname. Annual.
Contains a general review of the various sectors of the economy including banking and finance.

SWAZILAND

319. Monetary Authority of Swaziland. *Quarterly Review.* Mbabane, Swaziland, 1977– . Quarterly.
Reviews developments in the country's banking, finance, and foreign exchange.

SWEDEN

320. Sveriges Riksbank. Swedish National Bank. *Yearbook.* Stockholm, Sweden, 1908– . Annual.
Covers the banking and financial sector including the role of the central bank. Includes data on money, credit, interest rates, and foreign exchange. It is updated by the *Quarterly Review* (1979–). The country's statistical office (Statistika Sentrabyra) also publishes reports containing banking and monetary statistics, such as the monthly *Sparbankerna och föreningsbankerna* relating to savings banks.

SWITZERLAND

321. Banque nationale suisse. *Les banques suisses.* Zurich, Switzerland, 1920– . Annual.
Covers all financial institutions, their profits, losses, money, currency, credit, and international payments. The *Rapport annuel* and *Bulletin mensuel* contain similar information plus detailed statistical tables on foreign exchange, money supply, and interest rates. Developments in the country's banking system are covered in the annual *Das schweizerische Bankwesen im Jahre*. The Union Bank of Switzerland issues frequent statistical releases entitled *Foreign Exchange News* and an annual *Foreign Exchange Quotations* covering major world currencies.

322. Euromoney Publications. *Swiss Capital Markets.* London, England, 1985. 136p.
A comprehensive survey of the bond and equity markets, private placements, long-term credit equity, and mutual fund and money markets. Also includes details of the institutional and legal framework, banking system, taxes, the structure of holding companies, insurance, pension funds, and stock exchanges.

Foreign Country Sources 61

TANZANIA

323. Bank of Tanzania. *Economic and Operations Report.* Dar es Salaam, Tanzania. Annual.
>Reviews the country's monetary policies and includes statistical data on money, credit, and foreign exchange. More updated information is available from the quarterly *Economic Bulletin* (1969–).

THAILAND

324. Bank of Thailand. *Annual Economic Report.* Bangkok, Thailand, 1964– . Annual.
>Covers money, banking, foreign exchange, and gold price movements. Also reports on the bank's monetary policies. The annual is supplemented by the *Monthly Bulletin.*

TRINIDAD and TOBAGO

325. Central Bank of Trinidad and Tobago. *Quarterly Economic Bulletin.* Port-of-Spain, Trinidad and Tobago, 1976– . Quarterly.
>Reports on the central bank's activities, money supply, currency, commercial banking, and financial ratios. Banking statistics are also available in the monthly *Statistical Digest* and in the Central Statistical Office's annual *Financial Statistics.*

TUNISIA

326. Al-Bank al-Markazi al-Tunisi. Banque centrale de Tunisie. *Rapport d'activité.* Tunis, Tunisia, 1971– . Annual.
>In addition to a review of the central bank's activities, this publication provides data on the monetary situation and foreign exchange. A quarterly, *Ihsaiyat maliyah (Statistiques financières),* provides more detailed data on banking and finance.

UGANDA

327. Bank of Uganda. *Annual Report.* Kampala, Uganda, 1969/70– . Annual.
>Presents the activities of the central bank. Also covers banking laws and credit and monetary developments. The *Quarterly Bulletin* (1969–) also reviews the nation's financial situation.

UNITED KINGDOM

328. Bank of England. *Statistical Abstract.* London, England, 1975– . Annual.
>Contains statistics on banking, credit, external finance, capital and money markets, and interest and foreign exchange rates. The bank's monetary policy activities are covered in the annual *Report and Accounts.* Detailed statistics on the country's banking system and interest and exchange rates are available from the bank's *Quarterly Bulletin.* Other

bank publications in this area include the annual *U.K. Flow of Fund Accounts* and the weekly *Bank Return*.

329. Financial Times Business Information. *British Banking Directory*. London, England, 1986– . Annual.
Lists over 550 deposit-taking institutions with a financial summary of assets and liabilities for each.

URUGUAY

330. Banco central del Uruguay, Departamento de investigaciones economicas. *Reseña de la actividad economica-financiera*. Montevideo, Uruguay, 1981– . Annual.
This annual reviews the financial and monetary situation in the country. Similar topics are covered in the monthly *Boletín estadístico mensual* (1972–) and quarterly *Indicadores de la actividad economica-financiera*.

VENEZUELA

331. Banco central de Venezuela. *Boletín mensual*. Caracas, Venezuela, 1944– . Monthly.
A review of the financial situation in the country. A quarterly *Boletín trimestral* (1982–) covers the banking and monetary situation. An annual *Informe economico* (1962–) deals with financial and foreign exchange markets.

WEST GERMANY

332. Euromoney Publications. *German Bond Markets*. London, England, 1986. 170p.
The Deutsche Mark is the second most important Eurocurrency held by foreigners. This book describes the operation of German bond markets, including the banking system, the domestic bond market, certificates in indebtedness, the Euro-DM market in terms of financing instruments, and participants in the international German bond markets.

YEMEN

333. Central Bank of Yemen. *Annual Report*. Sanas, Yemen. Annual.
Includes information on money supply, banking, credit, currency, and foreign exchange. The quarterly *Financial Statistical Bulletin* (1973–) covers similar subjects.

YUGOSLAVIA

334. Narodna Banka Jugoslavije. National Bank of Yugoslavia. *Annual Report*. Belgrade, Yugoslavia. Annual.
A good source of information on the country's foreign exchange situation and domestic money supply. Supplementary data are available from the *Quarterly Bulletin*. Monetary statistics can also be found in the publications of Savezni zavod za statistiku (Federal Institute of Statistics in

Belgrade) such as the annual *Yugoslavia in Figures* and *Statistical Yearbook*.

ZAIRE

335. Banque du Zaire. *Rapport annuel.* Kinshasa, Zaire. Annual.
Covers banking, money, and credit. The bank also issues a *Bulletin mensuel de la statistique* (1974–) and *Bulletin trimestriel* (1961–) on the credit market and foreign exchange.

ZAMBIA

336. Bank of Zambia. *Annual Report.* Ndola, Zambia, 1970– . Annual.
Contains statistical tables on banking and the monetary situation in the country. Updated information is available from the *Quarterly Financial and Statistical Review* (1970–).

ZIMBABWE

337. Zimbabwe. Ministry of Finance. *Economic Survey.* Salisbury, Zimbabwe. Annual.
Data, provided by the Central Statistical Office, include the banking and financial sectors.

International Sources

338. American International Investment. *World Currency Charts*. San Francisco, CA, 1961.
Provides historical data on foreign exchange rates in terms of the U.S. dollar. Data are given in both charts and tables. In most cases, statistics go back to the early 1900s.

339. Amex Bank. *The Amex Bank Review*. London, England, 1973– . Monthly.
Regional and some country-by-country surveys of the world's foreign exchange and bond markets.

340. Asiamedia. *Asia Banking Almanac*. 6th ed. Philadelphia, PA, 1986– . Annual.
Lists all foreign and domestic banking, financial, and investment companies in the Asia-Pacific region. Includes balance sheet information, country of incorporation, and rankings. Formerly entitled *Asian Banking Directory*.

341. Association of International Bond Dealers. *International Bond Manual*. Zurich, Switzerland, 1978– . Annual.
Loose-leaf publication which covers international bonds, floating rate notes, and convertibles.

342. Aurora International. *Wrap-up on Latin American Banking and Finance*. Norwalk, CT, 1983– . Monthly.
Covers the monetary and financial situation in terms of money supply, interest rates, national debts, and other business indicators.

343. Bank Administration Institute. *Payment Systems in Eleven Developed Countries*, 2nd ed. Rolling Meadows, IL, 1985. 285p.
Presents payment practices in Belgium, Canada, France, Germany, Italy, Japan, Netherlands, Sweden, Switzerland, U.K., and U.S. Payment systems are compared by convenience, cost, security, and certainty.

344. Bank for International Settlements. *BIS Annual Report*. Basel, Switzerland, 1930– . Annual.
Surveys domestic credit markets and monetary situation around the world. Includes data on national currencies and world settlement patterns. The bank formerly published *International Banking Statistics* (1973–1983), which provided composite financial data on banks in the member nations. The annual report is supplemented by the monthly

International Banking and Financial Market Developments, which provides updated data. In addition, a semiannual, *The Maturity Distribution of International Bank Lending* deals with cross-border claims. The biannual publication entitled *The Maturity Distribution of International Bank Lending* (1985–) reports on total claims of reporting banks, new lending activity by country and region, lengthening of the maturity structure of outstanding claims, and debt rescheduling activities. The bank also publishes a monthly *International Banking and Financial Market Developments*, which includes the external position of banks in individual reporting countries, currency breakdowns of reporting banks' positions vis-à-vis nonresidents and residents, and the foreign currency position of reporting banks.

345. Bankers Publishing. *Bankers Almanac.* Boston, MA, 1986– . Annual.

Deals with trends and development in the banking community at state and national levels, with information compiled from over 70 sources. Contains data on interest rates, performance measures, and share of loans and deposits. In addition to a chronological recap of banking events in the preceding year, the almanac answers questions relating to annual asset growth and loan growth rates for banks; total volume of domestic office deposit rate by state; outstanding credit card balances; amounts of nonperforming loans and leases; and number of bank openings, closings, mergers, and consolidations. The almanac also contains summaries of state and federal banking laws plus a directory of trade associations and their activities.

346. Banque centrale des etats de L'Afrique de l'ouest. *Notes d'information et statistiques.* Dakar, Senegal.

Reviews the monetary situation in West African Monetary Union countries (Benin, Ivory Coast, Upper Volta, Niger, Senegal, and Togo).

347. Banque centrale des etats de L'Afrique equatoriale et du Cameroun. *Etudes et statistiques. Bulletin mensuel.* Paris, France, 1956– . Monthly.

Provides information on the monetary situation and banking activity for the African Monetary Union (Cameroon, Central African Empire, Gabon, and Chad).

348. Banques des etats de L'Afrique centrale. *Etudes et statistiques: Bulletin mensuel.* Paris, France, 1973– . Monthly.

Covers the Central African Republic, Congo, Gabon, and Chad. Includes banking statistics, money supply, and capital markets. The *Rapport annuel* provides similar data.

349. Barclays Bank. *Interest Rates.* London, England. Monthly.

Summary of the Eurodollar markets and national interest rates in Western European countries. The monthly *International Financial Survey* contains similar information.

350. Business International. *Business International.* New York, NY. Weekly.

In addition to the above, the corporation publishes a number of weekly publications, including *Business Europe, Business Latin America,* and

Business Asia, which contain reports on financial developments, currencies, and the outlook. The weekly *Money Report* features reports on currencies, foreign exchange markets and rates, and international bond markets.

351. Chadwick-Healy Inc. *Annual Reports from World's Central Banks.* Alexandria, VA, 1984– . Annual (microfiche).

This retrospective collection of annual reports covers the period 1946–1983. The subscription is kept up-to-date by new microfiche additions, at present covering 1984–1986. These reports are an important source of data on monetary policies, banking and treasury operations, currency, and foreign exchange.

352. Charles Fulton & Co. *Exchange Rate Databook.* London, England. Monthly.

Evaluates the monetary factors affecting key exchange rates and forecasts their movements. Covers the U.S. dollar, British pound, deutsche mark, Japanese yen, French franc, and Italian lira.

353. Citicorp Economic Services. *World Outlook: Five-Year Forecast, 1986–1990.* New York, NY. Annual.

The annual five-year forecast issue of Citicorp's *World Outlook* provides detailed forecasts on key economic, financial, and trade indicators for the world's top seven industrial countries: U.S., U.K., Japan, West Germany, France, Italy, and Canada. These countries account for over half of the world's economic activity, and they represent the most important markets for financial investments. *World Outlook*'s comprehensive but concise analyses serve as convenient references on current political and economic policies in each country. They present a consistent framework for market planning, investment analysis, risk evaluation, and strategic business decisions. Detailed annual forecast tables project economic growth, interest rates, inflation, currency exchange rates, and other major macroeconomic variables for each of these important countries. In addition, cross-country forecast tables allow one to compare developments in several countries at a glance.

354. Credit Suisse. *Credit Suisse Bulletin.* Zurich, Switzerland, 1971– . Quarterly.

National and international review of world stock exchanges, money and capital markets, foreign exchange and interest rates, and the gold market.

355. Economist Intelligence Unit. *Country Reports.* London, England, 1960– . Quarterly with annual supplements.

Formerly called the *Quarterly Economic Reviews of...*, these reports cover developments in virtually every country in the world. They are comprehensive examinations of the economic and financial scene in each country, containing both textual and tabular analyses. Data include money, banking, interest rates, and foreign exchange rates and reserves. These reports should be used for those countries where up-to-date information is hard to come by.

356. Euromoney Publications. *The Bank Register.* London, England. 1986– . (Annual)
The most complete and up-to-date directory of international and domestic financial institutions. Contains over 4,600 individual bank entries with the names and titles of 50,000 senior banking officers worldwide. Provides comprehensive details of specializations, shareholding, and balance sheet highlights. Gives a complete listing of each bank's subsidiaries and affiliates. Lists addresses and telephone and telex numbers of major branches and representative offices.

357. ———. *Bank Report.* London, England, 1986– . Monthly.
This publication tracks bank risk and performance in every country in the world. Reports on what is happening at any bank of any size anywhere and alerts the subscriber to danger signals at banks in countries where good information is scarce. Specially covered are all banks in the third world and smaller banks in developed countries. Includes data on bank performance, capital changes, banking laws and regulations, and correspondent banking.

358. ———. *Emerging Securities Markets.* London, England, 1986. 310p.
Contains a detailed analysis of the equity, bond, and money markets in Asia, the Middle East, Latin America, and Africa. Also covers the investment banking activities and practices in these countries. Provides detailed statistics on market size and activity, valuation, investors, regulation, and foreign portfolio investment.

359. ———, in association with Hambros Bank Ltd. *Euromarket Directory.* 4th ed. London, England, 1986. 700p.
This is a complete source of information on all borrowing organizations in the Euromarkets. Provides details on over 2,000 of the world's Euromarket debtor organizations in 120 countries, central banks, finance ministries, state corporations, supranational bodies, privately owned companies, and export credit agencies. Includes time series data for all borrowers in the syndicated loan market. Comprehensive information on each borrowing body covers names and addresses of the senior management responsible for borrowing, organizational relationships, stock ownership details, and nature of business. Subscription includes an updating service containing amendments to existing entries. Includes the following specific data: London dollar certificates of deposit; Euro commercial papers; gold, silver, and currency options; bullion; Eurobonds; floating rates; Eurocurrency deposits; syndicated bank credits; and Euronote facilities.

360. ———. *Euromoney Capital Markets Guide.* London, England, 1976– . Weekly.
Provides complete details on all financial instruments traded in the world's capital markets. Formerly called the *Euromoney Syndication Guide*, the weekly service also includes monthly and annual updates available by separate subscription. Each week complete details are included on Euronotes, RUFs and related facilities, syndicated loans, international bonds, renegotiations, project financings, and export credits. Also contains a section on country volume and market breakdown by the type of instrument.

361. ———. *Euromoney Corporate Finance.* London, England. Monthly.

Provides detailed information for financial officers, whether in a corporation or bank, who need to keep abreast of the rapidly changing market in which they must operate. Covered in detail are fixed and floating rates, domestic and Euro; private placements; market conditions worldwide; availability of finance; regulations and controls; profiles; techniques and transactions; currency and interest rates; savings; terms and conditions of completed deals; pricing; the market makers; accounting and taxes; documentation; mergers and acquisitions; contested and agreed cross-border deals; the price and the financing; international equity issues, new listings; foreign ownership; market makers; share dealing systems; regulations and the Euro-equity market; cash management and venture capital; sources of funds; corporate and bank portfolios; and strategies and profiles. In addition there is a specially formulated databank of statistics providing critical figures on borrowing costs, yield and return data, hedging costs, and benchmark prices for currency and interest rate swaps.

362. ———. *Euromoney Currency Report.* London, England, 1979– . Monthly.

Designed for corporate treasurers whose company earnings are affected by fluctuations in foreign exchange rates. Each issue contains the following: forecast for nine major exchange rates, detailed analysis of the prospects for 15 major currencies, recommendations for hedging exposures in 19 different currencies, reports on minor currencies not covered by other services, short-term forecasts for key exchange rates, trends in currency and interest rate swap markets, and details of exchange control changes. Regular features include bond portfolio advice, currency polls, and supplementary information on key currency movements and long-term expectations for world's major currencies. Subscribers to this service can also get two special telex services providing up-to-the-minute information on volatile currency markets. Called "summary telex" and "alert telex," they analyze the latest developments affecting the major currencies.

363. ———. *Euromoney International Bond Annual.* London, England. Annual.

A complete record of international bond market activity. Contents include analysis of new borrowing instruments; list of hybrid bonds announced during the preceding year; lead manager and bookrunner analysis; tables by currency and by main categories of issuers, such as sovereign borrowers, public utilities, and corporations; analysis of all issues managed by top lead manager banks; analysis by country and by instrument; syndicated relationships; ranking of the biggest individuals; classification by economic and regional areas; average coupons and maturities; and a glossary of bond market terms.

364. ———. *Euromoney International Euronote and Loan Annual.* London, England. Annual.

Formerly *Euromoney International Loan Annual*, this directory provides a complete analysis of the Euronote market and the syndicated loan market, using the data from the Euromoney Capital Market's Guide Database. Contents include a complete listing of all Euronotes and RUFs issued today; rescheduling country lists, including terms, fees, and servicing banks; lead rankings and lead managers to major country borrowers and major economic groupings; analysis by country and interest rate type; and analysis by currency. The directory also includes a ranking of the top 100 individual borrowers.

365. ———. *Euromoney Mergers and Acquisitions Guide.* London, England, 1985– . Annual.

This is a complete record of mergers and acquisitions in the world-wide financial industry completed in the previous year, together with a comprehensive and thorough analysis of cross-border and national transactions. Contents include full names of institutions involved, value of the transaction, financing arrangements, summaries of tender offers, counter bids and blocking tactics, analysis of the 100 largest deals, analysis of the 50 largest cross-border deals, and a detailed country analysis.

366. ———. *Euromoney Trade Finance Report.* London, England. Monthly.

Discusses and explains the latest developments in trade and project finance worldwide. Contains data on sources of subsidized finance; export credit agencies and eximbanks; document collection and letters of credit; bills of exchange; countertrade; a forfäit; buyer credits; cofinancing; leasing and factoring; trading blocked funds; private export credit insurance; payments, regulations, and controls; the latest deals and projects; using options and futures; import finance; recourse and nonrecourse finance and guarantees; exchange risk policies; evaluating financing offers; contract guarantees and international bonding practices; electronic banking; energy; aircraft and shipping finance; and legal issues and documentation. This exhaustive monthly analysis is aimed at most export credit agencies and banks.

367. ———. *Euromoney Yearbook.* London, England, 1984– . Annual.

Provides detailed data on every aspect of international finance. Contains otherwise difficult to obtain information on changes in legal, fiscal, and accounting regulations affecting the operation of markets, banks, and other financial institutions. Contents include reports on developments affecting the operation of banks and corporations in the world's financial centers; detailed statistics on foreign exchange, including a four-year history of rates for 25 currencies; interest rates for 25 countries; country risk data for the 50 most important borrowers; and bond yields and equity return in 18 financial markets. Also includes information on default and renegotiation, electronic banking, futures, international bond and equity issues, leasing, mergers and acquisitions, options, swaps, syndicated loans, trade finance, and venture capital. The directory also provides key reference materials, such as a listing of international banks and companies, a comprehensive glossary, addresses of the world's most important financial associations, and a diary of forthcoming events.

368. ———. *International Capital Markets.* 3rd ed. London, England, 1986. 214p.

Contains comprehensive descriptions of the instruments available in the world's national and international money and capital markets. Includes such instruments as fixed interest bonds like Eurobonds, foreign and domestic bonds, fixed rate certificates of deposit, treasury bills, commercial papers, floating rates, securities, and domestic notes.

369. ——. *Telerate-Euromoney World Wide Directory of Foreign Exchange, Futures and Options Dealers.* London, England, 1985– . Annual.
Provides the most up-to-date, comprehensive list of foreign exchange dealers and managers, directors, and traders in futures and options and of banks, brokerage houses, corporations, and other financial institutions. Contents include a detailed guide to the currencies in which the institutions and dealers specialize and a list of the major international futures and options contracts traded by brokers and dealing rooms.

370. ——. *Treasury Report.* London, England, 1986– . Monthly.
This publication keeps corporate treasurers fully informed of borrowing costs, foreign exchange rate movements, interest rates, and currency exposures. Also includes information on futures and options, swap markets, hedging, and forecasts of key financial indicators. Subscribers can also get the latest foreign exchange rates and other money market developments through special telex updates.

371. ——. *World Money and Securities Markets.* London, England, 1986. 490p.
Contains a comprehensive summary of worldwide money and securities markets from the perspectives of the borrower and the investor. Indepth analyses for 30 countries include operations of money and capital markets, dealing costs and fees, withholding taxes and exchange controls, financial and monetary systems, and a record of recent market performance and activity.

372. European Economic Community. Savings Bank Group. *Report.* Brussels, Belgium, 1966– . Biennial.
Contains composite financial information and analyses of trends in the savings bank industry in the European Economic Community.

373. Extel Statistical Services. *Extel International Bonds Service.* London, England, 1970– . Weekly.
Loose-leaf service which surveys new and existing bonds listed on international markets and gives details on individual bonds including prospects and dates.

374. Financial Times. *International Reports.* London, England, 1986– . Weekly.
This is a new advisory service on all aspects of international finance, foreign exchange, country risk, and foreign regulations and laws. Each issue contains inside information gathered from world financial centers presented as anticipations, forecasts, and analyses along with a vast compendium of invaluable statistics. Anticipations are key developments in countries around the world and commentary on all aspects of banking finance and foreign exchange. Also includes foreign exchange projections, international interest rates, international loan syndication and bond markets, a statistical market letter, and monthly chart service. Data provided include official free and parallel market rates in foreign exchange for 97 countries; international money and capital market rates, with yields, for

22 currencies; a survey of arbitrage loan costs; and a complete cross-rate survey of major currencies.

375. ———. *Who Owns What in World Banking.* London, England, 1986– . Annual.
A guide to the subsidiary and affiliated interests of the world's largest banks, including multinational and consortium banks.

376. Financial Times Business Information. *Banking in the EEC: Structures and Sources of Finance.* London, England, 1985. 145p.
For each country covered, an explanation is provided of the banking and financial system and capital and money markets. Includes a directory of banks as well as over 50 tables of financial and banking statistics.

377. ———. *Banking in the Far East: Structures and Sources of Finance.* London, England, 1986. 152p.
Covers Australia, China, Hong Kong, Indonesia, Japan, Republic of Korea, Malaysia, New Zealand, the Philippines, Singapore, and Thailand. Includes a directory of banks in the region and over 40 tables of statistics relating to banking and other financial institutions as well as money and capital markets.

378. Global Management Bureau. *Debt Watch.* Toronto, Canada, 1984– . Bimonthly.
Newsletter devoted to an analysis of world debt patterns. Includes different levels of indebtedness, such as corporate, consumer, and national public debt.

379. Gold Institute. *Modern Gold Coinage.* Washington, DC, 1977– . Annual.
Reports on gold coins issued as money in 65 countries or world areas. Includes the number of gold coins issued, gold content, physical characteristics of coins, mints where coins are struck, total gold use, and total face value of coins in local currency for each country.

380. ———. *World Mine Production of Gold.* Washington, DC. Annual.
Report on underground, surface, and alluvial gold mine production in 57 countries. Data are from approximately 250 mining enterprises. Contains tables showing estimated and projected gold production by country and names and locations of participating companies, arranged by country.

381. Healey Centre for Forecasting. *Currency Profiles.* New York, NY: Manufacturers Hanover Trust, 1979– . Monthly.
Short-term and long-term forecasts of U.S. dollar rates against 17 other currencies, with commentaries on developments in each of the countries covered.

382. IC Publications. *Top African Banks.* London, England, 1984.
Provides data such as capitalization, administration and management, and balance sheet and income statements of individual banks in all African countries except South Africa.

383. Institute of International Finance. *Data Service.* Washington, DC, 1983– .
The IIF was established in 1983 by the world's leading commercial banks to improve the timeliness and quality of information available on sovereign borrowers. It provides online reports and customized data on borrowing countries to member banks. The data, however, are not available to nonmembers.

384. International Business Information. *Asia/Pacific Currency Report.* Cincinnati, OH, 1983– . Semimonthly.
Provides detailed analysis of the foreign exchange market and currency movement for Asia and Pacific region countries.

385. ———. *International Currency Report.* Cincinnati, OH, 1978– . Monthly.
Detailed analysis of world's major currencies and trends and developments in the foreign exchange markets.

386. International Currency Analysis. *World Currency Yearbook.* New York, NY, 1961– . Annual.
Previously entitled *Pick's Currency Yearbook*, this publication covers world monetary trends and developments. It presents detailed country-by-country data on currency in circulation, official currency exchange rates, black market rates, and gold prices. Includes data on Eurocurrency interest rates and gold supply and demand. A section entitled "Currency Overview" lists currency and trade areas and currency ownership restrictions. Currency profiles include a review of the currency's history, transferability, and lists of currency varieties and/or areas where the currency is used. The gold review includes profiles of gold trading countries and monthly prices of gold bullion, coins, futures, and contracts. There is also a directory of central banks. The annual is supplemented by the monthly *Pick World Currency Report*.

387. International Insider Publishing. *Who's Who in International Banking, 1986.* Philadelphia, PA: Taylor & Francis, 1986. Annual.
Biographical information published annually since 1984 on senior international bankers, listed by bank within geographical regions.

388. International Monetary Fund. *Annual Report on Exchange Arrangements and Exchange Restrictions.* Washington, DC, 1950– . Annual.
Survey of developments regarding foreign exchange restrictions country by country. Covers capital and gold movements.

389. ———. *International Finance Statistics.* Washington, DC, 1947– . Monthly.
This is a standard source of data on all aspects of domestic and international finance. Covers over 137 member countries. Statistics include exchange rates, international liquidity, money, banking, government finance, and interest rates. Frequent *Supplements on Exchange Rates* provide more detailed data on foreign exchange rates and SDRs. IMF's *Yearbook* updates this information and provides historical trends. The *Government Finance Statistics Yearbook* covers each member country's

revenue, expenditures, lending, financing, and public debt of the central government.

390. International Reports. *International Country Risk Guide.* New York, NY, 1980– . Monthly.
Provides detailed analysis by country of financial, monetary, and economic conditions as a guide to multinational investors.

391. ———. *International Reports.* New York, NY, 1947– . Weekly.
Contains detailed analysis of the movements in major currencies and foreign exchange markets.

392. International Savings Banks Institute. *Report.* Geneva, Switzerland, 1970– . Biennial.
Covers trends and developments in the savings bank industries in most countries. Provides composite data, such as number of institutions, loans, and deposits.

393. Middle East Economic Digest. *Middle East Financial Directory.* London, England, 1983– . Annual.
Also called *MEED/TAIC Middle East Financial Directory*. Lists financial and banking firms by area and country. Includes foreign branch banks and Middle Eastern banks with branches abroad. Published in cooperation with Bank Abu Zaby al-Watani.

394. Morgan Guaranty Trust. *Morgan Guaranty Survey.* New York, NY, 1961– . Monthly.
Covers current U.S. and international financial topics, including credit markets, Federal Reserve activities, and monetary policy. Includes data on monetary indicators, government finance, and outlook on credit markets.

395. ———. *Morgan International Data.* New York, NY. 6/yr.
Contains extensive statistics on real and nominal effective exchange rates, interest rates, money market rates, and international debt. Individual issues are crammed with important financial information on 90 countries around the world. This publication supplements a companion monthly, *World Financial Markets*.

396. ———. *World Financial Markets.* New York, NY, 1978– . Monthly.
Provides data on foreign exchange market developments and rates and domestic and international issues affecting financial markets. Feature articles on various aspects of world economy are supplemented by regular statistical tables in the appendix on nominal and effective exchange rates; real effective exchange rates; Eurocurrency market size, deposit rates, and bank credits; international bond yields; new international bond issues; central bank discount rates; day-to-day money rates, treasury bill rates, and representative money market rates; commercial bank deposit rates and lending rates to prime borrowers; and domestic, government, and corporate bond yields.

397. Organisation for Economic Cooperation and Development. *Financial Market Trends.* Paris, France. 3/yr.
Covers major domestic and international financial markets of the OECD countries. Provides comprehensive statistics on internationally syndicated Eurocredits, international bank lending, Eurobonds and traditional foreign bond issues, interest rates, foreign exchange rates, and monetary and fiscal reviews of member countries. Includes a chronological listing of measures affecting financial markets. A companion publication, *Financial Statistics* is issued in three parts: Part 1, *Monthly Financial Statistics*, comes out in two sections and covers international and foreign bond issues and medium- and long-term loans, domestic security issues and lending transactions, and national and international interest rates. Part 2, *Financial Accounts*, issued twice a year, deals with the flow of funds accounts and the balance sheet accounts for 20 countries, broken down by institutional sectors and financial instrument. Part 3, *Non-Financial Enterprises Financial Statements*, an annual, covers the sources and uses of funds for enterprises in 12 countries. Banking and financial statistics are also available from other OECD publications, for instance, *Main Economic Indicators* (monthly and historical), *OECD Economic Surveys,* and *OECD Economic Outlook.*

398. Rand McNally. *International Bankers Directory.* Skokie, IL, 1872– . Annual.
Popularly known as the *Blue Book*, the directory contains financial information on all U.S. banks and their branches, arranged by state and city.

399. R.L. Polk Co. *Polk's World Bank Directory.* Nashville, TN, 1894– . Annual.
Published in two volumes, one covering national banks and the other international banks, this directory summarizes financial and related data on all the banks in the world. The national edition is arranged by state and city. The international edition is arranged by country and city.

400. Samuel Montagu & Co. *Annual Bullion Review.* London, England, 1936– . Annual.
Sometimes called *Annual Bullion Letter.* Surveys precious metal markets, especially gold and silver, with prices, holdings and reserves, treasury auctions, and futures markets.

401. Société Financière Européenne. *World Monetary Outlook.* Paris, France, 1972– . Biannual.
Published in cooperation with Barclay's Bank Ltd., this report covers the sources and uses of capital in Belgium, France, West Germany, Italy, Japan, Netherlands, Switzerland, U.K., and U.S.

402. St. Gall Institute of Banking Statistics. *Leading European Banks.* Berne, Switzerland, 1974– . Annual.
Formerly *100 European Banks*, this report provides a comparative financial analysis of 100 major banking institutions in Europe.

403. Thomas Skinner Directories. *The Bankers' Almanac and Yearbook.* West Sussex, England. Annual.

Contains two main sections, one on British and the other on international banks. In addition to directory information on each bank, the following data are included: capital structure, balance sheet, worldwide correspondents, subsidiaries, ownership, and history. Also included are geographical and alphabetical indexes, amalgamations and absorptions of British banks since 1700, and details on banking associations and on coins and notes of the world.

404. ———. *The Bankers' Almanac World Rankings.* West Sussex, England, 1986– . Annual.

Worldwide in scope, this almanac includes rankings of 2,000 international banks. They are listed alphabetically, showing their position, based on total assets, in the world and also in their country of registration. Over 150 individual countries are covered. The data are taken from individual banks' audited balance sheets. Only banks in the *Bankers' Almanac and Yearbook* are included. The figures are shown in U.S. dollars, but asset growth is based on national currencies.

405. Vallancy International. *Who's Who in Banking in Europe.* 3rd ed. Philadelphia, PA: Taylor & Francis, 1984. 1,200p.

Alphabetical entries give a broad range of information, including specializations in 12 different areas, on 30,000 European bankers. Separate indexes list banks geographically and individuals under general banking specializations.

406. Woodhead Faulkner. *Foreign Exchange Yearbook.* Cambridge, England. Annual.

Includes daily foreign exchange and Euromoney deposit rates for world's leading currencies.

407. World Bank. External Debt Division. Economic Analysis and Projections Dept. *World Debt Tables.* Washington, DC, 1978– . Annual.

Covers the public and private lending activities for developing countries and debt service operations, arranged by country and region. Updated by quarterly supplements.

408. ———. Financial Studies Division. Programming and Budgeting Dept. *Borrowing in International Capital Markets.* Washington, DC, 1974– . Quarterly with annual supplements.

Analysis and summary with statistical information on developments in world capital markets. Data include borrowings, international bonds, Euromoney credits, and Eurodollar deposit rates.

409. World Banking Intelligence. *World Banking Monitor.* New York, NY, 1984– . Monthly.

This is a newsletter for international banking executives and corporate loan and syndicated loan officers. Covers important facts and events in banking communities throughout the world. Includes information on new products and services, acquisitions and mergers, personnel changes and appointments, capital restructurings, and emerging forms of financial services and institutions.

410. World Council of Credit Unions. *International Credit Union Yearbook.* Madison, WI, 1954– . Annual.
Information on the financial condition and activities of credit unions in over 70 countries.

411. World Currency Report. *Pick World Currency Report.* New York, NY, 1955– . Monthly.
Provides monthly data on official and black market exchange rates for 96 foreign currencies against the U.S. dollar. Includes information on prices of precious metals and gems. In addition to analyses of world currency developments, statistical features and summary charts include the following: London daily silver spot prices and futures prices; Eurodollar and Eurosterling rates in London; gold prices in New York, London, Singapore, and Hong Kong; gold sales in international markets; and prices of silver and platinum.

412. World Reports Limited. *Gold and Silver Survey.* New York, NY, 1980– . Monthly.
This loose-leaf newsletter contains commentary and data on factors affecting the gold and silver markets. The text is supported by data on international gold and silver prices from 16 financial centers. Much of the information is also presented in charts.

413. ———. *Interest Rate Service.* New York, NY, 1977– . 15/yr.
Contains comprehensive survey of interest rate developments and changes in monetary policies in 21 important financial centers in the world. In addition to comprehensive data on interest rates, the service covers selected indicative rates for bonds and long-term government securities. Also contains a special interest rate chart section which presents a country-by-country visual record of interest rate developments. The following core countries are covered in each issue: U.S., U.K., West Germany, Japan, France, Switzerland, Netherlands, Belgium, Canada, Italy, Spain, Denmark, Norway, Sweden, Australia, South Africa, Hong Kong, and Singapore. Interest rate developments in other countries are also dealt with when they are significant.

414. ———. *International Currency Review.* New York, NY. 6/yr.
Reviews currency and exchange rate movements and monetary policies affecting same for major currencies. Also covers gold and silver market prices as they affect the currencies covered.

415. ———. *London Currency Report.* New York, NY, 1972– . 15/yr.
This loose-leaf report contains comprehensive foreign exchange commentary and financial intelligence of importance to the banking community and government agencies. The report consists of three sections: "World Currency Reports" gives running commentaries on global currency developments, "Exchange Rate Data Service" is a comprehensive and continuously updated survey of global exchange rate data, and "International Currency Charts" presents in an easy-to-read chart format data relating to exchange rate fluctuations.

416. ———. *Middle East Currency Reports.* New York, NY, 1974– . 8/yr.

These loose-leaf reports focus on financial and banking developments in Morocco, Tunisia, Algeria, Libya, Egypt, Jordan, Syria, Saudi Arabia, Qatar, Bahrain, Kuwait, United Arab Emirates, Oman, and the Yemens.

Databases

417. *American Banker.* New York, NY: American Banker Inc. and International Thomson Organization, 1980– . Updated daily. Vendor: Innerline.

Textual and numeric database containing daily news coverage and analyses of events and trends in the financial services industries.

418. *Australian Financial Database (COMERT 1).* Toronto, Canada: I.P. Sharp Associates, 1977– . Updated monthly. Vendor: I.P. Sharp.

Numeric database containing financial statistics from the Australian Bureau of Statistics and the Reserve Bank of Australia. Includes interest rates, trading banks, credit unions, finance companies, merchant banks, and permanent building societies. Government financial statistics include data on treasury notes, yields, money supply, and currency and capital flows.

419. *Australian Financial Markets (ARAYE).* Toronto, Canada: I.P. Sharp Associates, 1976– . Updated daily. Vendor: I.P. Sharp.

Textual and numeric database originating from the Commonwealth Trading Bank and Schroder Darling and Company. Includes interest and exchange rates, commercial and call loan rates, and promissory note and certificate of deposit rates.

420. *Australian Funds Markets (COMERT 3).* Sydney, Australia: Comert Business Economist, 1965– . Updated annually. Vendor: I.P. Sharp.

Textual and numeric database containing money supply and flow of funds data.

421. *Balance of Payments.* Washington, DC: International Monetary Fund, 1950– . Updated monthly. Vendor: Chase Econometrics.

A numeric database indicating long-term and short-term capital movements, foreign exchange reserves, and allocation of special drawing rights to member countries.

422. *Bancall.* Ann Arbor, MI: ADP Network Services, 1979– . Updated quarterly. Vendor: ADP Network Services.

Numeric database providing call report data taken from the FDIC reports. Covers all insured commercial banks and provides statements of their conditions and other composite financial data as well as information on mergers and acquisitions.

423. *Bancompare.* New York, NY: Cates Consulting Analysts, 1973– . Updated annually. Vendor: ADP Network Services.
    Numeric database taken from reports submitted to the FDIC, Federal Reserve Bank, and the Securities Exchange Commission. Contains financial statements on banks and bank holding companies.

424. *Bancshare.* Columbus, OH: Huntington National Bank, 1982– . Updated daily. Vendor: CompuServe.
    Textual and numeric database taken from bank computer files covering interest rates and bank news.

425. *Bank Analysis.* Atlanta, GA: Robinson-Humphrey-American Express, 1969– . Updated quarterly. Vendor: Control Data.
    Numeric database originating in reports submitted to federal regulatory agencies. Contains quantitative analysis of financial institutions, including peer group analysis and credit studies.

426. *Bank for International Settlements.* Toronto, Canada: I.P. Sharp Associates, 1979– . Updated quarterly. Vendor: I.P. Sharp.
    Numeric database taken from the Bank for International Settlements' files. Covers total liabilities and assets for about 200 countries.

427. *Bank of Canada Weekly Financial Statistics (WBANK).* Toronto, Canada: I.P. Sharp Associates, 1976– . Updated weekly. Vendor: I.P. Sharp.
    Taken from the Bank of Canada files, this numeric database provides weekly banking and monetary statistics, including money supply and interest rates and assets, liabilities, and liquidity of banks.

428. *Bank of England Databank.* London, England: The Bank, 1970– . Updated quarterly. Vendor: SIA Computer Services.
    This numeric database is taken from a variety of reports submitted to governmental and banking organizations. Contains information on discount rates, exchange rates, international interest rates, and rates on London money markets.

429. *Canadian Chartered Banks.* Toronto, Canada: I.P. Sharp Associates, 1981– . Updated monthly. Vendor: I.P. Sharp.
    Numeric database taken from individual Canadian banks. Provides statistics on total assets and liabilities, income, and stockholders' equity for all chartered banks.

430. *CEI Financial Forecast.* Claremont, CA: Claremont Economics Institute, 1984– . Updated weekly. Vendor: Claremont Economics Institute.
    Textual and numeric database containing forecasts of interest and inflation rates as well as foreign exchange rates.

431. *CITIBASE.* New York, NY: Citicorp Information Services, data vary depending on series. Updated daily. Vendor: I.P. Sharp Associates.
    Numeric database taken from reports submitted to federal regulatory agencies. Among other things contains time series data on interest rates, money supply, and exchange rates.

432. *Citicorp Economic Report.* New York, NY: Citicorp Information Services, date varies depending on series. Updated daily. Vendor: Reuters.

Full-text database originating in reports submitted to federal regulatory agencies and the bank's own research. Contains forecasts, analyses, and commentaries on the nation's monetary policy, business conditions, Treasury activity, and foreign exchange and interest rates.

433. *Conticurrency.* Chicago, IL: Conticurrency, 1976– . Updated daily. Vendor: Computer Sciences.

Textual and numeric full-text database providing brokerage quotes. Includes spot rates and forecasts for 40 currencies as well as projected exchange rates for 17 currencies. Also gives bonds and interest rates.

434. *Currency Exchange Database.* Rockville, MD: International Marine Banking Company, 1960– . Updated daily. Vendor: General Electric Information Services.

Numeric database containing current and historical data on world's most commonly used currencies.

435. *Currency Exchange Rates.* Toronto, Canada: I.P. Sharp Associates, 1965– . Updated daily. Vendor: I.P. Sharp.

Numeric database drawn from the world's leading commercial banks and from financial publications such as the *Financial Times*. Contains current and historical forward rates as well as spot exchange rates for major currencies on most active foreign-exchange markets.

436. *Daily Currency Report.* Boston, MA: Herman Communications, 1986– . Updated daily. Vendor: CompuServe.

Textual and numeric database providing information from the producer's phone survey and worldwide network of correspondents reporting on the interbank currency and futures markets.

437. *DRI Bank Analysis Service.* Washington, DC: Data Resources, Data Products Division, date varies depending on series. Updated continuously. Vendor: Data Resources.

Numeric database originating from the Board of Governors of the Federal Reserve System, Federal Deposit Insurance Corporation, and the Federal Home Loan Bank Board. Contains balance sheet and income statement data for individual savings and loans, mutual savings banks, and commercial bank holding companies throughout the U.S. and the territories of Guam and Puerto Rico.

438. *DRI Current Economic Indicators Data Bank (DRI-CEI).* Washington, DC: Data Resources, Data Products Division, date varies depending on series. Updated continuously. Vendor: Data Resources.

Numeric database on all countries includes data such as foreign exchange rates, trade-weighted rates and reserves, money supplies, and interest rates.

439. *DRI Financial and Credit Statistics Databank (DRI-FACS).* Washington, DC: Data Resources, Data Products Division, date varies depending on series. Updated continuously. Vendor: Data Resources.

Numeric database taken from reports submitted to federal regulatory agencies and databases of leading banks, such as Bank of America and Barclays Bank International, and financial services, such as Moody's Investors Service. Covers interest rates, financial data on commercial and thrift institutions, domestic money markets, Treasury securities, and foreign exchange markets.

440. *Electronic Yellow Pages: Financial Services Directory.* Westport, CT: Market Data Retrieval, 1986– . Updated biannually. Vendor: DIALOG.

Taken from the main electronic yellow pages, corporate and government reports, and mail and phone surveys, this directory gives the names, addresses, phone numbers, assets, and liabilities of banks, savings and loans, and credit unions.

441. *Eurabank.* Franklin Lakes, NJ: Sleigh Corporation, Eurastar Division, 1979– . Updated weekly. Vendor: Control Data.

Numeric database taken from the reports of the major central banks of the world, providing financial statistics of non–U.S. banks located in more than 100 countries. Individual bank data include consolidated statements of condition.

442. *Evans' Financial Database.* Washington, DC: Evans Economics, 1955– . Updated weekly. Vendor: Boeing Computer Services.

Numeric database taken from federal regulatory agencies and the files of commercial services such as Standard and Poor's. Contains time series information on consumer credit, commercial and industrial loans, interest rates, money supply, and assets and liabilities of commercial banks.

443. *Evans' Flow of Funds Database.* Washington, DC: Evans Economics, 1980– . Updated quarterly. Vendor: Boeing Computer Services.

Numeric database taken from the records of the Federal Reserve Board. Provides the flow of funds data which measures the aggregate stocks and flow transactions between the financial and nonfinancial markets for the various sectors of the U.S. economy.

444. *Evans' IMF Statistics Database.* Washington, DC: Evans Economics, 1980– . Updated monthly. Vendor: Boeing Computer Services.

Numeric data taken from the files of the International Monetary Fund. Statistics on more than 200 countries include exchange rates, international liquidity, money and banking, government finances, and interest rates.

445. *Evans' International Database.* Washington, DC: Evans Economics, 1960– . Updated weekly. Vendor: Boeing Computer Services.

Numeric database taken from various sources, such as the Organization for Economic Cooperation and Development. Includes time series data on government finances, banking and finance, and foreign exchange markets.

446. *External Debt Data Bank.* Washington, DC: Data Resources, Data Products Division, 1980– . Updated continuously. Vendor: Data Resources.
Numeric database taken from the records of the World Bank and the Bank for International Settlements. Contains statistics on the external public debt and financial position of developed and developing nations.

447. *FDIC.* Washington, DC: Federal Deposit Insurance Corporation, 1977– . Updated quarterly. Vendor: ADP Network Services.
Numeric database taken from the call and condition reports filed with federal regulatory agencies by commercial banks. Contains balance sheet and income statement data as well as composite financial data for over 15,000 commercial banks.

448. *Federal Reserve Board Weekly (FRBW).* Toronto, Canada: I.P. Sharp Associates, 1980– . Updated weekly. Vendor: I.P. Sharp.
This numeric database contains banking and monetary statistics released by the Federal Reserve System.

449. *Federal Reserve Week.* Silver Spring, MD: Business Publishers, 1981– . Updated weekly. Vendor: NewsNet.
Full-text database version of the hard copy *Federal Reserve Week*, which monitors the nation's monetary policy, interest rate movements, and international lending trends.

450. *Fedwatch.* Belmont, CA: Money Market Services, 1983– . Updated weekly. Vendor: CompuServe.
Full-text database version of the hard copy *Fedwatch*, which focuses on Federal Reserve activities, interest rate trends, money supply, and bank reserves.

451. *Financial.* Bala Cynwyd, PA: Chase Econometrics, 1980– . Updated weekly. Vendor: Chase Econometrics.
Numeric database taken from the records of the Federal Reserve System covering member bank's reserves and consolidated statements of condition, money supply, interest rates, commercial bank statistics, consumer credit, and savings institution data.

452. *Financial Forecast.* Bala Cynwyd, PA: Chase Econometrics, 1950– . Updated monthly. Vendor: Chase Econometrics.
Numeric database containing forecasts of interest rates, loans and deposits of commercial banks, monetary aggregates, Treasury operations, consumer credit, commercial paper, and savings and loans' activities.

453. *Financial Institute Database (FINDB).* New York, NY: Cates Consulting Analysts, 1974– . Updated monthly. Vendor: Control Data.
Numeric database taken from the reports filed with federal regulatory agencies. Contains consolidated condition reports and income statements for insured commercial banks, savings and loans, and credit unions.

454. *Flow of Funds (USFLOW)*. Washington, DC: Federal Reserve Board, 1952– . Updated quarterly. Vendor: ADP Network Services.
Numeric database provides seasonally adjusted data on the sources and uses of funds in different sectors of the U.S. economy.

455. *Foreign Exchange*. Bala Cynwyd, PA: Chase Econometrics, 1964– . Updated weekly. Vendor: Chase Econometrics.
Numeric database taken from the files of the International Monetary Fund and the *Financial Times*. Covers foreign exchange rates against the U.S. dollar for over 100 countries, expressed in both the national currency and U.S. dollars.

456. *Foreign Exchange (FX)*. Ann Arbor, MI: ADP Network Services, 1980– . Updated daily. Vendor: ADP Network Services.
Numeric database containing foreign exchange rates and domestic financial data for the world's advanced economies. Includes spot and forward rates; interest rates on Eurocurrency, London Interbank Offered Rates (Libor), and domestic money markets; and gold and silver prices.

457. *Foreign Exchange Database*. Waltham, MA: Interactive Data, 1977– . Updated daily. Vendor: Interactive Data.
Numeric database providing bid and asked quotations for spot and forward exchange rates for 16 currencies and interest rates for Eurocurrencies.

458. *Funds Marketplace (FUNDS)*. Arlington Heights, IL: Innerline, 1983– . Updated daily. Vendor: Innerline.
Numeric database taken from data provided to the Bank Administration Institute relating to the funds trading system. Indicates buy and sell offers for federal funds and other monetary instruments.

459. *German Bundesbank Monthly (BUNDESBANK)*. Frankfurt, West Germany: Deutsche Bundesbank, 1982– . Updated monthly. Vendor: I.P. Sharp Associates.
Numeric database containing data on German banks, including assets, liabilities, loans, and deposits.

460. *GNMA Data Base (GNMAX)*. Greenwich, CT: Control Data, 1980– . Updated monthly. Vendor: Control Data.
Numeric database taken from the records of the Government National Mortgage Association. Provides descriptive information on pooled mortgage-backed passed-through securities.

461. *Government Finance Statistics*. Washington, DC: International Monetary Fund, 1980– . Updated monthly. Vendor: Chase Econometrics.
Numeric database relating to revenues, grants, net lending, domestic and foreign financing, and debt operations of member countries.

462. *Government Securities Management System (GSMS)*. New York, NY: Lloyd Bush and Associates, 1979– . Updated monthly. Vendor: Lloyd Bush.
Textual and numeric database taken from government agencies. Provides information on mortgage-backed securities from GNMA, FNMA, and

FHLMC. Includes information on unpaid balances, payoff speeds, prices, yields, and accrued interest.

463. *Insight.* Belmont, CA: Money Market Services, 1982– . Updated monthly. Vendor: CompuServe.

Full-text database version of the hard copy *Insight*. Based on records of federal regulatory agencies as well as research from The Institute of Economic and Monetary Affairs. Provides forecasts on interest rates, money supply, and foreign exchange rates.

464. *International Financial Statistics.* Washington, DC: International Monetary Fund, date varies depending on series. Updated monthly. Vendor: Chase Econometrics and others.

Numeric database version of the hard copy *International Financial Statistics*. Deals with interest and exchange rates, international liquidity, money, banking, and government finances in member countries.

465. *MIDS/Banking and Finance.* Dallas, TX: Marketing Information Data Systems, 1980– . Updated annually. Vendor: General Electric Information Services.

Numeric database taken from the records of federal regulatory agencies. Contains aggregates on commercial banks, credit unions, and savings and loans.

466. *Money Market Monitor.* Arlington Heights, IL: Innerline, 1982– . Updated weekly. Vendor: Innerline.

Numeric database based on phone surveys conducted on behalf of the Bank Administration Institute. Covers interest rates for different types of bank accounts, analyzed nationally, regionally, by bank size, and by trend.

467. *Money Market Rates (MRATE).* Toronto, Canada: I.P. Sharp Associates, 1979– . Updated daily. Vendor: I.P. Sharp.

Numeric database taken from the world's major financial publications. Provides daily and weekly money market rates for several countries, prime rates, dollar swaps, treasury bills, certificates of deposit, banker's acceptances, commercial paper, mortgage rates, call loans, discount rates, and other negotiable instruments. Also gives foreign exchange rates for major currencies.

468. *Money Market Services Inc.* Belmont, CA: Money Market Services, Institute of Economic and Monetary Affairs, 1977– . Updates continuously. Vendor: Telerate.

Textual and numeric database taken from government records as well as research by analysts. Forecasts interest and foreign exchange rates.

469. *Money Markets Database.* Waltham, MA: Interactive Data, 1977– . Updated daily. Vendor: Interactive Data.

Numeric database providing information on interest rates for all money market instruments.

470. *Moneywatch.* New York, NY: McCarthy, Crisanti & Maffei, 1986– . Updated daily. Vendor: Quotron Systems and others.

Textual and numeric database version of hard copy *Money Market Critique*. Contains interest rate forecasts as well as monetary statistics.

471. *Mortgage Index.* Roslyn, NY: Hale Systems, 1978– . Updated continuously. Vendor: Hale Systems.
   Numeric database version of hard copy *Mortgage Index Newsletter.* Presents data taken from government and private agencies on nationwide mortgage market activity.

472. *Prime Rates.* Arlington Heights, IL: Innerline, 1982– . Updated irregularly. Vendor: Innerline.
   Textual and numeric database originating in surveys by the Bank Administration Institute. Provides past and current prime interest rates and broker prime lending rates.

473. *Probe Database of FOREX Rates.* New York, NY: Global Finance Information, 1977– . Updated daily. Vendor: RAPIDATA.
   Numeric database providing spot and forward exchange rates for major currencies and rates for Eurodollar deposits.

474. *Savings and Loans.* Washington, DC: Federal Home Loan Bank Board, 1977– . Updated biannually. Vendor: ADP Network Services.
   Numeric database taken from the records of federal regulatory agencies. Provides financial statistics on insured savings and loans.

475. *Scan.* Roslyn, NY: Hale Systems, 1979– . Updated quarterly. Vendor: Hale Systems.
   Textual and numeric database taken from the records of the Federal Home Loan Bank Board. Provides financial data on insured savings and loans, including industry trends, peer group analysis, and merger activities.

476. *Trustcompare.* New York, NY: Cates Consulting Analysts, 1982– . Updated monthly. Vendor: Control Data.
   Numeric database which gives analytical financial ratios for the trust departments of commercial banks.

477. *United States Banks (USBANKS).* Toronto, Canada: I.P. Sharp Associates, 1984– . Updated quarterly. Vendor: I.P. Sharp.
   Numeric database taken from the Federal Reserve Board reports on balance sheets and income statements for insured commercial banks.

478. *United States Bonds (USBOND).* Toronto, Canada: I.P. Sharp Associates, 1983– . Updated daily. Vendor: I.P. Sharp.
   Numeric database taken from the Associated Press. Covers daily trading activity of U.S. Government securities.

479. *Weekly Economic and Foreign Exchange Survey.* Belmont, CA: Money Market Services, 1984– . Updated weekly. Vendor: Dow Jones News/Retrieval and CompuServe.
   Contains forecasts of financial, capital, credit, and foreign exchange markets.

480. *Y9.* Washington, DC: Federal Reserve Board, 1978– . Updated biannually. Vendor: ADP Network Services.
   Numeric database taken from the annual reports submitted to the Federal Reserve System by bank holding companies.

Directory of Publishers

ADP Network Services
175 Jackson Plaza
Ann Arbor, MI 48106

Advertising News Research
Box 08888
North Palm Beach, FL 33408

Alabama. Department of Banking
64 N. Union St., Rm 651
Montgomery, AL 36130

Alaska. Department of Commerce
  and Economic Development
Pouch D
Juneau, AK 99811

American Banker Inc.
1 State Street Plaza
New York, NY 10004

American Express International
  Banking Corp.
Trafalgar House, 11 Waterloo Pl.
London SW1Y 4AS England

Arizona. Banking Department
1601 W. Jefferson, Rm 101
Phoenix, AZ 85007

Arkansas. Bank Department
No. 1 Capitol Mall, Rm 4B-210
Little Rock, AR 72201

Asiamedia Co. Ltd.
2 Wellington St. 16/F
Hong Kong

Association of Bank Holding
  Companies
730 15th St. N.W.
Washington, DC 20005

Bangladesh Bank
Department of Public Relations and
  Publications
Head Office, Motijheel Commercial
  Area
P.O. Box 325
Dacca, Bangladesh

al-Bank al-Markazi al-Misri
Central Bank of Egypt
31 Kasr El Nil St.
Cairo, Egypt

al-Bank al-Markazi al-Tunisi
Banque Centrale de Tunisie
7 Place de la Monnaie
Tunis, Tunisia

American Banker Association
1120 Connecticut Ave. N.W.
Washington, DC 20036

American Financial Services
  Association
4th Floor, 1101 4th St. N.W.
Washington, DC 20005

Association of International Bond
  Dealers
Universitat Strasse 105
CH-8033
Zurich, Switzerland

Aurora International
Box 9099
Bridgeport, CT 06601

BCA Publications Ltd.
3463 Peel St.
Montreal PQ H3A 1W7 Canada

Banco Central de Bolivia
Departmento de Estudios
  Economicos
Sucursal No. 1
La Paz, Bolivia

Banco Central de Chile, Santiago
Santiago de Chile
Agustinas 1180, P.O. Box 967
Santiago, Chile

Banco Central de Costa Rica
Division de Asuntos Economicos
Ave. Central y Primera
Colles 2-4, P.O. Box 10058
San José, Costa Rica

Banco Central de Honduras
Departmento de Estudios
  Economicos
1A Calle 6A & 7A Avenida
P.O. Box C-58
Tegucigalpa DC
Honduras CA

Banco Central de la Republica
  Dominicana
Calle Pedro Henriques Urena
Santo Domingo, Dominican
  Republic

Banco Central de Nicaragua
Apartado 2252
Managua, D. N.
Nicaragua

Banco Central de Reserva del Peru
Jiron A Miro Quesade 445
P.O. Box 1958
Lima, Peru

Banco Central de Venezuela
Esquina de Carmelitas
Avenida Urdaneto P.O. Box 2017
Caracas, Venezuela

Banco Central del Ecuador
Secretaria General
AV 10 de Agosto y Briceno Plaza
  Bolivar
P.O. Box 339
Quito, Ecuador

Banco Central del Paraguay.
  Departmento de Estudios
  Economicos
Avda Pablo VI y Avda Sargento
  Marecos
P.O. Box 861
Asuncion, Paraguay

Banco Central del Uruguay
Departmento de Investigaciones
  Economicas
Montevideo, Uruguay

Banco Central do Brasil.
  Departmento Economico
CP 04-0170
70.000 Brasilia DF, Brasil

Banco de Angola
Rua da Prata 10
Lisboa 2
Lisbon, Portugal

Banco de Espana
Alcala 50
Central Madrid 14
Madrid, Spain

Banco de Guatemala
7A Avenida 22-01
Zona 1
Guatemala City, Guatemala

Colombia. Banco de la Republica
Carrera 7a
No. 14-78
Bogota, Colombia

Bank Administration Institute
60 Gould Center
Rolling Meadows, IL 60008

Bank al-Maghrib. Banque du Maroc
287 Avenue Mohamed V
Rabat, Morrocco

Bank al-Sudan
Sharin El Gamaa
P.O. Box 313
Khartoum, Sudan

Bank for International Settlements
Centralbahnplatz 2
CH4002 Basel, Switzerland

Bank Indonesia
Urusan Ekonomi dan Statistik Jalan
   Kebon Sirih 82-84
Jakarta, Indonesia

Bank of Afghanistan. Research
   Department
Ibne Sina Wat
Kabul, Afghanistan

Bank of Botswana
P.O. Box 712
Gaborone, Botswana

Bank of Canada
245 Sparks St.
Ottawa, ON K1A 0G9 Canada

Bank of England
Economic Intelligence Department
Threadneedle St.
London EC2R 8AH England

Bank of Ghana. Board of Directors
P.O. Box 2674
Accra, Ghana

Bank of Guyana
P.O. Box 1003
Georgetown, Guyana

Bank of Sierra Leone
Westmoreland St.
Freetown, Sierra Leone

Bank of Tanzania
P.O. Box 2939
Dar es Salaam, Tanzania

Bank of Thailand. Department of
   Economic Research
Bang Khunprom
Bangkok Metropolis, Thailand

Bank of Uganda
37/43 Kampala Rd.
P.O. Box 7120
Kampala, Uganda

Bank of Zambia
P.O. Box 80
Lusaka, Zambia

Bank Yisrael. Bank of Israel
Research Department
Kiryat Ben Gurion
P.O. Box 780
Jerusalem, Israel

Bankcard Holders of America
333 Pennsylvania Ave. S.E.
Washington, DC 20003

Banker's Desk Reference
210 South St.
Boston, MA 02111

Bankers Digest Inc.
6440 N. Central Expressway
Dallas, TX 75206

Bankers Publishing Co.
210 South St.
Boston, MA 02111

Bankers Research Inc.
12 Avery Pl.
Westport, CT 06880

Bankers Trust Co.
P.O. Box 318
Church St. Station
New York, NY 10015

Banque Centrale des Etats De
   L'Afrique de L'ouest
Avenue du Barachois
Daka, Senegal BP 3108

Banque Centrale des Etats de
   L'Afrique et du Cameroun
29 rue du Colisee
75008 Paris, France

Banque de la Republique du
   Burundi
BP 705
Bujumbura, Burundi

Banque du Zaire
Bd Colonel Tshatshi
Kinshasa
BP 2.697 Zaire

Banques des Etats de L'Afrique
   Centrale
29 rue du Colisee
75008 Paris, France

Barclays Bank Ltd.
Group Economic Intelligence Unit
54 Lombard St.
London EC3P 3AH England

Business International Corp.
1 Dag Hammarskold Plaza
New York, NY 10017

Business Publishers Inc.
951 Pershing Dr.
Silver Spring, MD 20910

CCH Canadian Ltd.
6 Garamond Ct.
Don Mills, ON M3C 125 Canada

California. Banking Department
235 Montgomery St.
San Francisco, CA 94104

Canadian Bankers Association
P.O. Box 282
Toronto Dominion Centre
Toronto, ON M5K 1K2 Canada

Canadian Payments Association
50 O'Connor, Ste. 1212
Ottawa, ON K1P 6L2 Canada

Cates Consulting Analysts Inc.
74 Trinity Pl.
New York, NY 10006

Central Bank of Barbados
Research Department
P.O. Box 1016
Bridgetown, Barbados

Central Bank of China
21 Paoching Rd.
Taipei, Taiwan

Central Bank of Cyprus
P.O. Box 1087
Nicosia, Cyprus

Central Bank of Iraq
Statistics and Research Department
Rashid St., P.O. Box 64
Baghdad, Iraq

Central Bank of Nigeria, Lagos
Tinubu Square
PMB 12194
Lagos, Nigeria

Central Bank of Somalia
P.O. Box 11
Mogadishu, Somalia

Central Bank of the Bahamas
P.O. Box 4868
Nassau, Bahamas

Central Bank of the Gambia
1-2 Buckle St.
Banjul, Gambia

Central Bank of Trinidad and
   Tobago
Independence Square
P.O. Box 1250
Port of Spain, Trinidad and Tobago

Central Bank of Yemen
Ali Abd Al-Moghni St.
P.O. Box 59
Sanas, Yemen

Centrale Bank van Suriname
Waterkant 20 P.O. Box 1801
Paramaribo, Suriname

Chase Econometric Associates Inc.
555 City Line Ave.
Bala-Cynwyd, PA 19004

Chicago Board of Trade
LaSalle at Jackson
Chicago, IL 60604

The Chicago Corp.
208 LaSalle
Chicago, IL 60601

Chicago Mercantile Exchange
30 S. Wacker Dr.
Chicago, IL 60606

Citicorp Information Services
399 Park Ave.
P.O. Box 5294, FDR Station
New York, NY 10150

Claremont Economics Institute
415 W. Foothill Blvd.
Claremont, CA 91711

Colorado. Department of
   Regulatory Agencies
303 W. Colfax Ave., Ste. 700
Denver, CO 80204

Comert Business Economist Ltd.
Carlton Centre, 8th Floor
55 Elizabeth St.
2000 Sydney, NSW Australia

Commodity Exchange Inc.
4 World Trade Center
New York, NY 10048

Communication Channels Inc.
6255 Barfield Rd.
Atlanta, GA 30328

Directory of Publishers 91

The Conference Board
845 3d Ave.
New York, NY 10022

Conference of State Bank
  Supervisors
1015 18th St. N.W., Ste. 606
Washington, DC 20036

Connecticut. Department of
  Banking
44 Capitol Ave.
Hartford, CT 06106

Consulton Ltd.
522 Colomb Rd.
Singapore 6

Conticurrency Inc.
1800 Board of Trade Bldg.
Chicago, IL 60604

Control Data Corp.
Bas Information Service
500 W. Putnam Ave.
P.O. Box 7100
Greenwich, CT 06836

Credit Suisse
Paradeplatz 8
CH-8021
Zurich, Switzerland

Credit Union National Association
5710 Mineral Point Rd.
Madison, WI 53701

Crittenden Publishing Inc.
P.O. Box 1150
Novato, CA 94948

Cyrus J. Lawrence Inc.
115 Broadway
New York, NY 10006

Data Resources Inc.
29 Hartwell Ave.
Lexington, MA 02173

Delaware, Department of
  Administrative Services
P.O. Box 1401
Dover, DE 19903

Deutsche Bundesbank
50 Wilhelm-Epstein Strasse 14
P.O. Box 3611
6 Frankfurt am Main 1
Frankfurt, West Germany

Dun and Bradstreet
3 Century Dr.
Parsippany, NJ 07054

Ernst & Whinney
153 E. 53d
New York, NY 10022

Euromoney Publications
Nestor House
Playhouse Yard
London EC4V 5EX England

Evans Economics Inc.
2120 L St., Ste. 510
Washington, DC 20037

Extel Statistical Services Ltd.
37-45 Paul St.
London EC2A 4PB England

Federal Deposit Insurance Corp.
550 17th St. N.W.
Washington, DC 20429

Federal Home Loan Bank Board
1700 G. St. N.W.
Washington, DC 20552

Federal Home Loan Bank of
  Atlanta
1475 Peachtree St. N.E.
Atlanta, GA 30348

Federal Home Loan Bank of Boston
1 Financial Center, 20th Floor
Boston, MA 02111

Federal Home Loan Bank of
  Chicago
111 E. Wacker Dr., Ste. 800
Chicago, IL 60601

Federal Home Loan Bank of
  Cincinnati
2000 Atrium II
221 E. 4th St.
Cincinnati, OH 45202

Federal Home Loan Bank of Dallas
500 E. John Carpenter Fwy.
Irving, TX 75062

Federal Home Loan Bank of Des
  Moines
907 Walnut
Des Moines, IA 50309

Federal Home Loan Bank of
    Indianapolis
South Tower, 1350 Merchants Plaza
115 W. Washington
Indianapolis, IN 46204

Federal Home Loan Bank of New
    York
1 World Trade Center, Floor 103
New York, NY 10048

Federal Home Loan Bank of
    Pittsburgh
1 Riverfront Center
20 Stanwix St.
Pittsburgh, PA 15222

Federal Home Loan Bank of San
    Francisco
600 California
San Francisco, CA 94108

Federal Home Loan Bank of Seattle
1501 4th Ave.
Seattle, WA 98101

Federal Home Loan Bank of
    Topeka
No. 3 Towsite Plaza
120 E. 6th St.
Topeka, KS 66603

Federal Home Loan Mortgage
    Corp.
1776 G. St. N.W.
Washington, DC 20013

Federal Reserve Bank of Atlanta
104 Marietta St. N.W.
Atlanta, GA 30303

Federal Reserve Bank of Boston
600 Atlantic Ave.
Boston, MA 02106

Federal Reserve Bank of Chicago
230 S. LaSalle
Chicago, IL 60604

Federal Reserve Bank of Cleveland
E. 6th St. & Superior Ave.
Cleveland, OH 44101

Federal Reserve Bank of Dallas
Akard & Wood Sts., Station K
Dallas, TX 75222

Federal Reserve Bank of Kansas
    City
925 Grand
Kansas City, MO 64198

Federal Reserve Bank of
    Minneapolis
250 Marquette Ave.
Minneapolis, MN 55480

Federal Reserve Bank of New York
Fed Reserve P.O. Station
New York, NY 10045

Federal Reserve Bank of
    Philadelphia
100 North 6th St.
Philadelphia, PA 19106

Federal Reserve Bank of Richmond
P.O. Box 27622
Richmond, VA 23261

Federal Reserve Bank of San
    Francisco
P.O. Box 7702
San Francisco, CA 94120

Federal Reserve Bank of St. Louis
Box 442
St. Louis, MO 63166

Federally Insured Financial
    Institutions
5100 Wisconsin Ave. N.W.
Washington, DC 20016

Financial Publishing Co.
86 Brookline Ave.
Boston, MA 02215

Financial Times
Bracken House, Cannon St.
London EC4P 4BY England

First National Bank of Chicago
Business and Economic Research
    Division
1 First National Plaza
Chicago, IL 60670

Florida. Office of the Comptroller
Division of Banking
The Capitol Bldg.
Tallahassee, FL 32301

Futures Industry Association
1825 Eye St., N.W. Ste. 1040
Washington, DC 20006

Georgia. Department of Banking and Finance
2990 Brandywine Rd., No. 200
Atlanta, GA 30341

Global Management Bureau
22 College St., Ste. 107
Toronto, ON M5G 1K2 Canada

Gold Institute
1026 16th St. N.W., Ste. 101
Washington, DC 20036

Golembe Associates Inc.
1025 Thomas Jefferson St. N.W., Ste. 301
Washington, DC 20007

HSN Consultants, Inc.
2218 Main
Los Angeles, CA 90007

Hale Systems Inc.
1044 Northern Blvd.
Roslyn, NY 11576

Handy and Harman
850 3d Ave.
New York, NY 10003

Hawaii. Division of Financial Institutions
1010 Richards St.
Honolulu, HI 96813

Herman Communications Corp.
107 South St.
Boston, MA 02111

Huntington National Bank
41 S. High St.
Columbus, OH 43287

IC Publications
69 Great Queen St.
London WC2 England

I. P. Sharp Associates
2 First Canadian Pl.
Exchange Tower, Ste. 1900
Toronto, ON M5X 1E3 Canada

Idaho. Department of Finance
700 W. State St.
Boise, ID 83720

Illinois. Commissioner of Banks and Trust Companies
Reisch Bldg, Rm 400
Springfield, IL 62701

Illinois. Department of Financial Institutions
421 E. Capitol
Springfield, IL 62701

Indiana. Department of Financial Institutions
1024 State Office Bldg.
Indianapolis, IN 46204

Innerline
95 W. Algonquin Rd.
Arlington, IL 60005

Institute of International Finance
2000 Pennsylvania Ave. N.W., Ste. 8500
Washington, DC 20006

Institutional Investor
488 Madison Ave.
New York, NY 10022

Interactive Data Corp.
486 Tottenham Pond Rd.
Waltham, MA 02154

International Business Information Inc.
P.O. Box 3218
Cincinnati, OH 45201

International Currency Analysis
7239 Ave. N.
Brooklyn, NY 11234

International Monetary Fund
Publication Unit
700 19th St. N.W.
Washington, DC 20431

International Reports Inc.
200 Park Ave. S.
New York, NY 10003

International Savings Banks Institute
I-3, rue Albert-Gos
CH 1206 Geneva, Switzerland

Investment Company Institute
1600 M Street N.W.
Washington, DC 20036

Iowa Department of Banking
Liberty Bldg.
Des Moines, IA 50319

Irving Trust Co.
Economic Research and Planning
  Division
1 Wall St. 11th Floor
New York, NY 10015

Japan Ministry of Finance
1-1, 3-chome
Kasumigaseki-Chiyoda-Ku
Tokyo, Japan

Kansas Banking Department
700 Jackson St.
Topeka, KS 66603

Kentucky. Department of Banking
  and Securities
911 Leawood Dr.
Frankfort, KY 40601

Law Bulletin Publishing Co.
415 N. State St.
Chicago, IL 60610

Lloyd Bush and Associates
156 William St.
New York, NY 10024

Louisiana. Department of
  Commerce
P.O. Box 94095
Baton Rouge, LA 70804

Magyar Nezeti Bank. National Bank
  of Hungary
Box 54, Szabadsag-ter 8-9
Budapest V, Hungary.

Maine. Department of Business
Occupational and Professional
  Regulation
State House, Station No. 36
Augusta, ME 04333

Manufacturers Hanover Trust Co.
Economic Department
350 Park Ave.
New York, NY 10022

Manufacturers Hanover Bank
Healey Centre for Forecasting
350 Park Ave.
New York, NY 10022

Market Data Retrieval
Ketchum Pl.
Westport, CT 06880

Marketing Information Data
  Systems Inc.
13531 N. Central Expressway,
  Ste. 2131
Dallas, TX 75243

Maryland Department of Licensing
  and Regulation
34 Market St., Ste. 800
Baltimore, MD 21202

McCarthy, Crisanti & Maffei, Inc.
71 Broadway
New York, NY 10006

McFadden Business Publications
6196 Crooked Creek Rd
Norcross, GA 30092

McGraw-Hill Economics
  Department
1221 Ave. of the Americas
New York, NY 10020

Michigan. Department of
  Commerce Financial Institutions
  Bureau
P.O. Box 30224
Lansing, MI 48909

Middle East Economic Digest
21 John St.
London WC1N 2BP England

Minnesota. Department of
  Commerce Division of Financial
  Institutions
5th Floor, Metro Square Bldg.
St. Paul, MN 55101

Mississippi Bankers Association
P.O. Box 37
640 North State St.
Jackson, MS 39205

Mississippi. Department of Banking
  and Consumer Finance
1206 Woolfolk Bldg.
Jackson, MS 39201

Monetary Authority of Singapore
SIA Building, 77 Robinson Rd.
Singapore 1

Monetary Authority of Swaziland
P.O. Box 456
Mbabane, Swaziland

Money Market Services Inc.
490 El Camino Rd.
Belmont, CA 94002

Montana. Commissioner of
  Financial Institutions
1424 9th Ave.
Helena, MT 59620

Moody's Investors Services Inc.
99 Church St.
New York, NY 10007

Morgan Guaranty Trust Co.
23 Wall St.
New York, NY 10015

Mortgage Bankers Association of
  America
1125 15th St. N.W.
Washington, DC 20005

Muassasat al-Naqd al Arabi al
  Saudi
Saudi Arabian Monetary Agency
  Research and Statistics
  Department
Riyadh, Saudi Arabia

Narodny Bank
Flat 2, Kursovoj perenlok 1/1
Moscow, USSR 119034

National Consumer Finance
  Association
1000 16th St., N.W.
Washington, DC 20036

National Council of Savings
  Institutions
1101 15th St., N.W.
Washington, DC 20005

National Federation of Independent
  Business
Capital Gallery E., Ste. 695
600 Maryland Ave., S.W.
Washington, DC 20024

Nebraska Department of Banking
  and Finance
301 Centennial Mall S.
P.O. Box 95006
Lincoln, NE 68509

De Nederlandsche Bank. NV
Westeindel 1
1017 ZN Amsterdam-Postbus 98
1000 AB Amsterdam, Netherlands

Nepal Rastra Bank. Central Office
Research Department
Baluwatar
Kathmandu, Nepal

New Hampshire Banking
  Department
97 N Main St.
Concord, NH 03301

New Jersey. Department of Banking
36 W. State St.
Trenton, NJ 08625

New Mexico. Regulation and
  Licensing Department
Financial Institutions Division
Lew Wallace Bldg.
Santa Fe, NM 87503

Norges Bank
P.O. Box 336
Sentrum, Oslo 1, Norway

North Carolina. Commissioner on
  Banks
430 N. Salisbury
Raleigh, NC 27611

North Dakota. Department of
  Banking and Financial
  Institutions
13th Floor, State Capitol
Bismarck, ND 58505

Northwestern Banker Co.
1535 Linden St., No. 201
Des Moines, IA 50509

Oklahoma Banking Department
4100 N. Lincoln Blvd.
Oklahoma City, OK 73105

Oregon. Department of Commerce
280 Coint St.
Salem, OR 97310

Organisation for Economic
  Corporation and Development,
  Paris
2 rue Andre-Pascal
75775 Paris, Cedex 16, France

Pennsylvania. Department of
   Banking
333 Market St., 16th Floor
Harrisburg, PA 17101

Purcell, Graham & Co.
61 Broadway
New York, NY 10027

R. L. Polk Co.
2001 Elm Pike
Nashville, TN 37210

Rand McNally & Co.
8255 N. Central Park
Skokie, IL 60076

Reserve Bank of India. Central
   Office
P.O. Box 1036
Bombay 400001, India

Reserve Bank of New Zealand
P.O. Box 2498
Wellington 6000
Wellington, New Zealand

Rhode Island. Department of
   Business Regulations
100 N. Main St.
Providence, RI 02903

Robert Morris Associates
1616 Philadelphia National Bank
   Bldg.
Philadelphia, PA 19107

Robinson-Humphrey-American
   Express
3333 Peachtree Rd.
Atlanta, GA 30326

Salomon Brothers Inc.
1 New York Plaza
New York, NY 10004

Samuel Montague & Co.
114 Old Broad St.
London EC2 England

Snaullah Publications
P.O. Box 4185
Karachi, Pakistan

Savers Advisory Service
Box 143520
Coral Gables, FL 33114

Securities Industries Association
120 Broadway, 35th Floor
New York, NY 10271

SeElabanki Islands. Central Bank of
   Iceland
Hafnarstraeti 20
Rejkjavik, Iceland

Shawmut Bank of Boston
1 Federal St.
Boston, MA 02110

Sheshunoff & Co.
P.O. Box 13203
Capitol Station
Austin, TX 78711

Silver Institute
1026 16th St. N.W., Ste. 101
Washington, DC 20036

Sleigh Corp.
Eurastar Division
P.O. Box 591
Franklin Lakes, NJ 07417

Societe Financiera Europeenne
20 Rue de la paix F-75002
Paris, France

South African Reserve Bank
Church Square
P.O. Box 427
Pretoria 0001, South Africa

South Dakota. Division of Banking
   and Finance
1st Floor, State Capitol
Pierre, SD 57501

Sri Lanka Maha Bankuva. Central
   Bank of Ceylon
Central Bank Bldg.
Colombo 1, Ceylon

Stanley Publishing
P.O. Box 689
Westboro, MA 01581

State Bank of Pakistan
Public Relations Department
   Post Box No. 4456
Karachi, Pakistan

Statistics Canada
Publications Distribution
Ottawa, ON K1A 0T6 Canada

Sunscape International Inc.
1513 E. Livingston
Orlando, FL 32803

Suomen Pankki. Bank of Finland
Institute for Economic Research
Helsingfors 10, Helsinki
Finland

Sveriges Riksbank
P.O. Box 16283
S-103 25 Stockholm
Stockholm, Sweden

T. C. S. Capital Management Inc.
2560 1st Ave.
San Diego, CA 92103

T. C. S. Enterprise Inc.
3878 Old Town Ave.
San Diego, CA 92110

T. K. Sanderson Inc.
200 E. 25th St.
Baltimore, MD 21218

Tennessee. Department of Financial Institution
James K. Polk Bldg., 2d Floor
Nashville, TN 37219

Thomas Skinner Directories Ltd.
Windsor Court
East Grinstead House
West Sussex RH19 1XE England

Trust Companies Association of Canada
335 Bay St., 7th Floor
Toronto, ON M5H 2R3 Canada

U.S. Board of Governors of the Federal Reserve System
20th & Constitution Ave., N.W.
Washington, DC 20551

U.S. Bureau of Mint
633 3d St. N.W.
Washington, DC 20220

U.S. Department of Agriculture
Agricultural Service
14th & Independence Ave. S.W.
Washington, DC 20250

U.S. Department of Treasury
15th & Pennsylvania Ave. N.W.
Washington, DC 20220

U.S. Federal Financial Institutions Examination Council
Ste. 701., 1776 G. St. N.W.
Washington, DC 20006

U.S. Government National Mortgage Association
451, 7th St. S.W.
Washington, DC 20414

U.S. Language of Savings Associations
111 E. Wacker Dr.
Chicago, IL 60601

U.S. Office of the Comptroller of Currency
490 L'Enfant Plaza S.W.
Washington, DC 20219

U.S. Savings Bonds Division
1111, 20th St. N.W.
Washington, DC 20226

Utah. Department of Financial Institutions
160 E. 300 S.
Salt Lake City, UT 84110

Veribanc, Inc.
116 Foundry
Woburn, MA 01801

Vermont. Department of Banking and Insurance
120 State St.
Montpelier, VT 23219

Virginia. Corporation Commission. Bureau of Financial Institution
13th Floor, Jefferson Bldg.
Richmond, VA 23219

Warren, Gorham & Lamont
210 South St.
Boston, MA 02111

Washington. Department of General Administration
Banking Division
218 General Administration Bldg.
Olympia, WA 98504

Wisconsin. Office of the Commissioner of Banking
P.O. Box 7876
123 Washington
Madison, WI 53707

World Bank. Financial Studies
   Division
Programming and Budgeting
   Department
1813 H St. N.W.
Washington, DC 20433

World Council of Credit Unions
5710 Mineral Point Rd.
Madison, WI 53701

World Reports Ltd.
280 Madison Ave., Ste. 1209
New York, NY 10016

Zimbabwe. Ministry of Finance
P.O. Box 7705
Harare, Zimbabwe

Title Index

References are to entry numbers not page numbers.

ABA Bank Card Letter, 80
ATM Cost Model, 90
ATM Directory, 91
Abridged Version of the Report of the Year..., Presented by the Governor to the Ordinary General Meeting of the Shareholders (Banca d'Italia), 276
Abstract of Condition (Montana, Commissioner of Financial Institutions), 28
Abstract of Condition (Oregon, Department of Commerce), 37
Afghan Financial Statistics, 228
Agricultural Credit Conditions Survey, 69
Agricultural Letter (Federal Reserve Bank of Chicago), 65
Agriculture: An Eighth District Perspective, 74
All Bank Statistics, United States, 1896-1955, 192
American Bank Directory, 149
American Banker, 79, 417
American Bankers Association Key to Routing Numbers, 174
American Savings Directory, 150
The Amex Bank Review, 339
Analysis of Bank Marketing Expenditures, 89
Annuaire statistique (Benin), 239
Annual Abstract of Statistics (Belize), 238
Annual Bullion Letter, 400
Annual Bullion Review, 400

Annual Digest of Statistics. St. Johns, Antigua, 230
Annual Economic Report (Bank of Thailand), 324
Annual Economic Report (South African Reserve Bank), 313
Annual Report (Alaska, Director of Banking, Securities and Corporations Division), 2
Annual Report (Bahrain Monetary Agency), 234
Annual Report (Banco nacional de Mexico), 293
Annual Report (Bangladesh Bank), 235
Annual Report (Bank of Botswana), 241
Annual Report (Bank of Guyana), 266
Annual Report (Bank of Iraq), 273
Annual Report (Bank of Israel), 275
Annual Report (Bank of Korea), 314
Annual Report (Bank of Mauritius), 292
Annual Report (Bank of Negera, Malaysia), 290
Annual Report (Bank of Sudan), 317
Annual Report (Bank of Uganda), 327
Annual Report (Bank of Zambia), 336
Annual Report (Central Bank of Iceland), 270
Annual Report (Central Bank of Ireland), 274

Annual Report (Central Bank of Jordan), 282
Annual Report (Central Bank of Libya), 287
Annual Report (Central Bank of the Philippines), 305
Annual Report (Central Bank of Yemen), 333
Annual Report (Florida), 9
Annual Report (Georgia), 10
Annual Report (Idaho), 12
Annual Report (Illinois), 13
Annual Report (Monetary Authority of Singapore), 311
Annual Report (National Bank of Liberia), 286
Annual Report (National Bank of Yugoslavia), 334
Annual Report (Norges Bank), 300
Annual Report (of Bureau of Financial Institutions, Virginia), 46
Annual Report (of Commissioner on Banks, North Carolina), 34
Annual Report (of Federal Home Loan Bank Board of Atlanta), 51
Annual Report (of Federal Home Loan Bank Board of Boston), 52
Annual Report (of Federal Home Loan Bank Board of Chicago), 53
Annual Report (of Federal Home Loan Bank Board of Cincinnati), 54
Annual Report (of Federal Home Loan Bank Board of Dallas), 55
Annual Report (of Federal Home Loan Bank Board of Des Moines), 56
Annual Report (of Federal Home Loan Bank Board of Indianapolis), 57
Annual Report (of Federal Home Loan Bank Board of New York), 58
Annual Report (of Federal Home Loan Bank Board of Pittsburgh), 59
Annual Report (of Federal Home Loan Bank Board of San Francisco), 60
Annual Report (of Federal Home Loan Bank Board of Seattle), 61
Annual Report (of Federal Home Loan Bank Board of Topeka), 62
Annual Report (of Federal Home Loan Bank Board of Washington, DC), 122
Annual Report (of Federal Reserve Bank of Atlanta), 63
Annual Report (of Federal Reserve Bank of Chicago), 65
Annual Report (of Federal Reserve Bank of Cleveland), 66
Annual Report (of Federal Reserve Bank of Dallas), 67
Annual Report (of Federal Reserve Bank of Kansas City), 68
Annual Report (of Federal Reserve Bank of Minneapolis), 69
Annual Report (of Federal Reserve Bank of New York), 70
Annual Report (of Federal Reserve Bank of Philadelphia), 71
Annual Report (of Federal Reserve Bank of Richmond), 72
Annual Report (of Federal Reserve Bank of St. Louis), 74
Annual Report (of Federal Reserve Bank of San Francisco), 73
Annual Report (of Financial Institutions, Illinois), 14
Annual Report (of Financial Institutions, Indiana), 16
Annual Report (of Financial Institutions, Minnesota), 24
Annual Report (of Financial Institutions Bureau, Michigan), 23
Annual Report (of Financial Institutions Division, New Mexico), 32
Annual Report (of National Credit Union Administration, Washington, DC), 167
Annual Report (of Superintendent of Banks, New York), 33

Annual Report (of the Commissioner of Banking, Wisconsin), 48
Annual Report (of the Department of Banking, Pennsylvania), 38
Annual Report (of the Department of Banking and Consumer Finance, Mississippi), 25
Annual Report (of the Department of Banking and Finance, Nebraska), 29
Annual Report (of the Department of Financial Institutions, Tennessee), 41
Annual Report (of the U.S. Comptroller of the Currency), 212
Annual Report (of U.S. Board of Governors of the Federal Reserve System), 193
Annual Report (Österreichische National Bank, Austria), 232
Annual Report (Saudi Arabian Monetary Agency), 308
Annual Report (U.S. Government National Mortgage Association), 221
Annual Report and Statement of Accounts (Central Bank of Nigeria), 299
Annual Report and Statement of Accounts (Central Bank of Somalia), 312
Annual Report and Statement of Accounts: Central Bank of Malta, 291
Annual Report: Central Bank of Kenya, 284
Annual Report of Superintendent of Banks of the State of Alabama, for the Fiscal Year Ending September, 1
Annual Report of the Bank Commissioner (Maryland), 22
Annual Report of the Bank Commissioner (New Hampshire), 30
Annual Report of the Bank Commissioner (Vermont), 45
Annual Report of the Banking Commissioner (Connecticut), 7
Annual Report of the Banking Division (Rhode Island), 39
Annual Report of the Board of Directors (Cyprus), 255
Annual Report of the Commissioner (Kentucky), 19
Annual Report of the Commissioner (New Jersey), 31
Annual Report of the Consumer Finance Companies (Arizona Banking Department), 3
Annual Report of the Director of the Mint, 210
Annual Report of the Directors and Statement of Accounts (Reserve Bank of New Zealand), 297
Annual Report of the Governor to the Minister of Finance and Statement of Accounts (Canada), 244
Annual Report of the State Bank Commissioner (Colorado), 6
Annual Report of the State Bank Commissioner (Delaware), 8
Annual Report of the Superintendent of Banking (Iowa), 17
Annual Report of the Superintendent of Banks (California), 5
Annual Report of the Supervisor of Banking (Washington), 47
Annual Report on Exchange Arrangements and Exchange Restrictions, 388
Annual Report on Operations and Accounts (Nepal Rastra Bank), 295
Annual Report on the Working of the Reserve Bank and Trend and Progress of Banking in India, 271
Annual Report Presented to the Banking Superintendent (Chile), 251
Annual Reports from World's Central Banks, 351
Annual Statistical Digest (Central Bank of Barbados), 236
Annual Statistical Digest (of U.S. Board of Governors of the Federal Reserve System), 194
Annual Statistical Report of the Bureau of Banking (Maine), 21
Annual U.S. Economic Data, 74

Anuario de fiscales y financieras (Colombia), 253
Anuário estatístico (Angola), 229
Applied Economics for Card Systems, 173
Arab Banking and Finance Handbook, 307
Arsberetning (Denmark), 256
Arthika vivaranya (Central Bank of Ceylon), 316
Asia Banking Almanac, 340
Asia/Pacific Currency Report, 384
Asian Banking Directory, 340
Asset and Liability Trends (Federal Home Loan Bank Board, Washington, DC), 123
Australian Financial Database (COMERT-1), 418
Australian Financial Markets (ATAYE), 419
Australian Funds Markets (COMERT 3), 420
Austria's Monetary Situation, 232
Availability and Sale of Foreign Currencies to U.S. Tourists and Citizens, 215

BIS Annual Report (Bank for International Settlements), 344
Balance (Honduras), 267
Balance mensual (Banco de Guatemala), 265
Balance of Payments, 421
Bancall, 422
Bancompare, 423
Bancshare, 424
Bangladesh Bank Bulletin, 235
Bank Acquisition Report, 187
Bank Analysis, 425
Bank Analysts Quarterly Handbook, 177
Bank and Quotation Record, 170
Bank Credit Analyst (Canada), 245
Bank Credit Card Balances and Repayment Habits, 171
Bank Credit Card Observer, 171
Bank Crime Statistics, 134
Bank Directory of New England, 76
Bank Expansion Quarterly, 142
Bank Facts: Chartered Banks of Canada, 247
Bank for International Settlements, 426

Bank Holding Companies of the United States, 183
Bank Holding Company Facts, 88
Bank Holding Company Research Report, 225
Bank Letter, 145
Bank of Canada Weekly Financial Statistics (WBANK), 427
Bank of England Databank, 428
The Bank of Your State, 183
Bank Officer Cash Compensation Survey, 92
Bank Operating Statistics, 116
Bank or Savings and Loan Research Report, 225
Bank Rate Monitor, 78
Bank Ratings of All U.S. Banks, 183
The Bank Register, 356
Bank Report, 357
Bank Return (Bank of England), 328
Bankcard Consumer News, 99
Bankers Almanac, 345
The Banker's Almanac and Yearbook, 403
The Bankers' Almanac World Rankings, 404
Banker's Desk Reference, 100
Banker's Diary and Guide, 226
Banker's Digest (Texas), 42
Banker's Research, 101
Banking (Reserve Bank of Australia), 231
Banking and Finance: An Eighth District Perspective, 74
Banking and Monetary Statistics, 195
Banking Directory of Canada, 249
Banking in the EEC: Structures and Sources of Finance, 376
Banking in the Far East: Structures and Sources of Finance, 377
Banking, Insurance and Other Private Finance, 231
Banking Statistics of Pakistan, 302
Banks and Financial Institutions in Singapore: The Consulton Report, 310
Bilans des banques (France), 262
Blue Bank Report, 225
Boletim (Banco central do Brasil), 242
Boletim trimestral (Angola), 229

Boletim trimestral (Brazil), 242
Boletín (Banco central de reserva del Peru), 304
Boletín (Banco central del Ecuador), 258
Boletí de estadísticas (Ecuador), 258
Boletín de estadísticas bancarias (Banco de Guatemala), 265
Boletín económico (Banco de España), 315
Boletín estadístico (Banco central de Chile), 251
Boletín estadístico (Banco central de Honduras), 267
Boletín estadístico (Banco central del Paraguay), 303
Boletín estadístico (Banco de España), 315
Boletín estadístico (Banco de Guatemala), 265
Boletín estadístico (Banco nacional de Mexico), 293
Boletín estadístico (Bolivia), 240
Boletín estadístico bancario (Banco central de reserva del Peru), 304
Boletín estadístico mensual (Banco central del Uruguay), 330
Boletín estadístico mensual (Costa Rica), 254
Boletín estadístico: Series historicas (Banco de España), 315
Boletín mensual (Banco central de Venezuela), 331
Boletín mensual (Chile), 251
Boletín mensual (Dominican Republic), 257
Boletín semestral (Nicaragua), 298
Boletín trimestral (Banco central de Venezuela), 331
Bolletino (Banca d'Italia), 276
Borrowing in International Capital Markets, 408
British Banking Directory, 329
Bulletin (Baghdad, Iraq), 273
Bulletin (Banque nationale du Rwanda), 306
Bulletin (Central Bank of Ceylon), 316
Bulletin (Central Bank of Somalia), 312
Bulletin (State Bank of Pakistan), 302

Bulletin de la banque nationale de Belgique, 237
Bulletin économique et financier (Belgium), 237
Bulletin mensuel (Bank of Lebanon), 285
Bulletin mensuel (Banque nationale du Cambodge), 283
Bulletin mensuel (Banque nationale suisse), 321
Bulletin mensuel (Burundi), 243
Bulletin mensuel de la statistique (Banque du Zaire), 335
Bulletin of Financial Statistics (Japan), 281
Bulletin trimestriel (Banque du Zaire), 335
Bulletin trimestriel (Burundi), 243
Bulletin trimestriel (France), 262
Bulletin trimestriel (Luxembourg), 288
Business Asia, 350
Business Europe, 350
Business Forecasts, 72
Business International, 350
Business Latin America, 350
Business Review (Federal Reserve Bank of Philadelphia), 71

CB Review (Central Bank of Philippines), 305
CD Investors Guide to Key Financial Ratios of All FSLIC Insured Savings and Loans, 188
CEI Financial Forecast, 430
COMEX Statistical Yearbook, 105
CUNA Yearbook, 110
Canadian Banker, 244
Canadian Chartered Banks, 429
Canadian Financial E-Z Directory, 248
Canadian Financial Institutions, 246
Change in Kansas State Banks for the Month of..., 18
Checks Cashed (Canada), 244
Chicago Banks, 15
CITIBASE, 431
Citicorp Economic Report, 432
City Five or County Five Report, 225
Coinage Executed, 211

Coins, 210, 211, 379
Combined Financial Statements (Federal Home Loan Bank Board, Washington, DC), 124
Commercial Bank Activities (Central Bank of Nigeria), 299
Comparative Abstract (Kansas), 18
Comparative Abstract (of the Division of Banking and Finance, South Dakota), 40
Comparative Statement of Assets, Liabilities, and Capital Accounts of Alaska Banks, 2
Comparative Statement of Condition (Hawaii), 11
Compte rendu: Banque de France, 262
Condensed Statement of Reports of State and Federal Savings and Loan Associations (Arizona), 3
Condensed Statement of Reports of State and National Banks of Arizona, 3
Confidential Bank Insurance Survey, 81
Consolidated Reports of Condition and Income (Federal Reserve Bank of Richmond), 72
Constant Prepayment Rate Yield Tables, 178
Consumer Credit Delinquency Bulletin, 82
Consumer Finance (Direct Cash Lending) Company Ratios, 137
Conticurrency, 433
Conventional Home Mortgage Rates, 125
Cost of Personal Borrowing in the United States, 136
Council Annual Report (U.S. Federal Financial Institutions Examination Council), 220
Country Exposure Lending Survey (Federal Financial Institutions Examination Council), 120
Country Exposure Lending Survey (U.S. Board of Governors of the Federal Reserve System), 196
Country Reports, 355
Credit and Capital Markets, 102
Credit Suisse Bulletin, 354

Credit Union Report, 109
Credit Unions (Canada), 244
Crédito y cuentas monetarias (Costa Rica), 254
The Crittenden Directory, 111
Cross Sections (Federal Reserve Bank of Richmond), 72
Cuadros estadísticos (Dominican Republic), 257
Currency Exchange Database, 434
Currency Exchange Rates, 435
Currency Profiles, 381

DRI Bank Analysis Service, 437
DRI Current Economic Indicators Data Bank (DRI-CEI), 438
DRI Financial and Credit Statistics Databank, (DRI-FACS), 439
Daily Currency Report, 436
Das schweizerische Bankwesen im Jahre (Banque national suisse), 321
Data Bank: Operating Banks and Branches, 117
Data Service (Institute of International Finance), 383
Debt watch, 378
Delinquency Rates on Bank Installment Loans, 82, 83
Depository Institutions Performance Directory, 227
The Desktop Bank Directory, 175
Developments in the Nigerian Economy, 299
Directory (of National Council of Savings Institutions), 165
Directory of American Financial Institutions, 151
Directory of American Savings and Loan Associations, 189
Directory of Canadian Trust Companies, 250
Directory of Financial Institution (Singapore), 311
Directory of Mutual Savings Banks of United States, 185
Directory of Trust Institutions, 106
District Data Highlights (Federal Home Loan Bank of Dallas), 55
District Economic Conditions (Federal Reserve Bank of Minneapolis), 69

Diversified Finance Company Ratios, 138
Domestic and International Commercial Loan Charge-offs, 176

Economic and Financial Review (Central Bank of Kenya), 284
Economic and Financial Review (Central Bank of Nigeria), 299
Economic and Financial Statistics Review (Bank al-Sudan), 317
Economic and Financial Survey of Angola, 229
Economic and Housing Indicators (Federal Home Loan Bank of San Francisco), 60
Economic and Operations Report (Bank of Tanzania), 323
Economic Bulletin (Bank of Guyana), 266
Economic Bulletin (Bank of Tanzania), 323
Economic Bulletin (Central Bank of Libya), 287
Economic Bulletin (Norges Bank), 300
Economic Bulletin of the National Bank of Hungary, 269
Economic Indicators (Federal Home Loan Bank of Topeka), 62
Economic Outlook (Irving Trust), 147
Economic Perspective (Federal Reserve Bank of Chicago), 65
Economic Review (Bank of Sierra Leone), 309
Economic Review (Federal Reserve Bank of Atlanta), 63
Economic Review (Federal Reserve Bank of Cleveland), 66
Economic Review (Federal Reserve Bank of Dallas), 67
Economic Review (Federal Reserve Bank of Richmond), 72
Economic Review (Federal Reserve Bank of San Francisco), 73
Economic Statistics Annual (Bank of Japan), 279
Economic Statistics Monthly (Bank of Japan), 279
Economic Survey (Bangladesh), 235
Economic Survey (Central Bank of Kenya), 284
Economic Survey (Zimbabwe), 337
Economic Trends (Federal Reserve Bank of Cleveland), 66
Economic Trends and Cycles (Federal Home Loan Bank of Cincinnati), 54
Electronic Funds Transfer System, 97
Electronic Yellow Pages: Financial Services Directory, 440
Emerging Securities Markets, 358
Estadística bancaria (Dominican Republic), 257
Estados financieras (Dominican Republic), 257
Estatísticas tributárias básicas (Brazil), 242
Estimated Member Information (Federal Home Loan Bank of Atlanta), 51
Estudio económico y memoria de labores (Banco de Guatemala), 265
Etudes et statistiques (Morocco), 294
Etudes et statistiques. Bulletin mensuel (Banque centrale des etats de L'Afrique equatoriale et du Cameroun), 347
Etudes et statistiques: Bulletin mensuel (Banques des etats de L'Afrique centrale), 348
Eurabank, 441
Euromarket Directory, 359
Euromoney Capital Markets Guide, 360
Euromoney Corporate Finance, 361
Euromoney Currency Report, 362
Euromoney International Bond Annual, 363
Euromoney International Euronote and Loan Annual, 364
Euromoney Mergers and Acquisitions Guide, 365
Euromoney Trade Finance Report, 366
Euromoney Yearbook, 367
Evans' Financial Database, 442
Evans' Flow of Funds Database, 443
Evans' IMF Statistics Database, 444
Evans' International Database, 445

Exchange Rate Databook, 352
Extel International Bonds Service, 373
External Debt Data Bank, 446

FDIC, 447
FDIC Annual Report, 118
Fact Book of the Philippine Financial System, 305
Factbook, 162
Factbook (Chartered Banks of Canada), 247
Factbook (Federal Home Loan Bank of Boston), 52
Faisnésis ráithiúil (Central Bank of Ireland), 274
Federal Reserve Board Weekly (FRBW), 448
Federal Reserve Bulletin, 197, 199
Federal Reserve Chart Book, 201
Federal Reserve Statistical Releases, 199
Federal Reserve Week, 449
Fedwatch, 450
Finance Corporation Statistics, 231
Finance Fact Yearbook, 87
Financial, 451
Financial and Economic Review (Reserve Bank of Malawi), 289
Financial Capital Flows and Stocks (Canada), 244
Financial Data (Federal Reserve Bank of St. Louis), 133
Financial Digest, 148
Financial Economist, 135
Financial Flow Accounts (Canada), 244
Financial Forecast, 452
Financial Indicators and Corporate Financing Plans, 107
Financial Information Report, Quarterly Report Aggregates (Federal Home Loan Bank of Indianapolis), 57
Financial Institute Database (FINDB), 453
Financial Institutions Financial Statistics (Canada), 244
Financial Letter (Federal Reserve Bank of Kansas City), 68
Financial Market Trends, 397
Financial Markets Weekly, 147

Financial Report on Colorado State Charter Savings and Loan Associations, 6
Financial Reporting Trends: Banking, 115
Financial Statements and Operating Ratios for the Mortgage Banking Industry, 154
Financial Statistical Bulletin (Central Bank of Yemen), 333
Financial Statistics (Barbados), 236
Financial Statistics (Central Bank of Trinidad and Tobago), 325
Financial Statistics of Japan, 281
Finanz-Compass Österreich, 232
Fjarmalatioinde (Financial Review) (Central Bank of Iceland), 270
Flow of Fund Accounts, 198
Flow of Funds (USFLOW), 454
Flow of Funds: Accounts, Assets and Liabilities Outstanding, 199
Foreign Currencies Held by U.S. Government, 216
Foreign Exchange, 455
Foreign Exchange (FX), 456
Foreign Exchange Database, 457
Foreign Exchange News (Banque nationale suisse), 321
Foreign Exchange Quotations (Banque nationale suisse), 321
Foreign exchange rates, 338, 339, 350, 352, 353-55, 369, 370, 371, 374, 381, 384, 385, 386, 406, 411. See also Currency movements.
Foreign Exchange Statistics (Bank of Korea), 314
Foreign Exchange Yearbook, 406
Foreign Lending Exposure Reports, 225
Freddie Mac Reports, 131
Functional Cost Analysis, 200
Funds Marketplace (FUNDS), 458
Funds Transfer Bank Contact Directory, 97

GNMA Data Base (GNMAX), 460
German Bond Markets, 332
German Bundesbank Monthly (BUNDESBANK), 459
Gold and Silver Survey, 412
Government Finance Statistics, 461

Government Finance Statistics Yearbook, 389
Government Securities Management System (GSMS), 462

Highlights (Federal Home Loan Bank of Cincinnati), 54
Historical Chart Book, 201
Holding Company Member Report, 225
Home Mortgage Commitment Rates in Illinois, 53
Home Mortgage Commitment Rates in Wisconsin, 53

IBJ Monthly Report (Bank of Japan), 279
IMF Yearbook, 384
Ihsaiyat maliyah (Statistiques financières) (Banque centrale de Tunisie), 326
Income and Expenses (Federal Reserve Bank of Richmond), 72
Index of Bank Performance, 93
Index Report (Federal Home Loan Bank of Chicago), 53
Indicadores de la actividad economica-financiera (Banco central del Uruguay), 330
Indicadores económicos (Banco nacional de Mexico), 293
Individual Bank Profiles, 94
Información estadística (Ecuador), 258
Informe anual (Banco central de Nicaragua), 298
Informe Anual (Banco de España), 315
Informe economica (Banco central de Venezuela), 331
Insight, 463
Installment/Consumer Credit Report, 84
Insured Savings and Loan Institutions' Savings by County in Illinois and Wisconsin, 53
Interest Rate and Metals Futures Statistical Annual, 103
Interest Rate Service, 413
Interest Rates, 349
International Bankers Directory (Blue Book), 398

International Banking and Financial Market Developments, 344
International Banking Statistics, 344
International Bond Manual, 341
International Capital Markets, 368
International Country Risk Guide, 390
International Credit Union Yearbook, 410
International Currency Report, 385
International Currency Review, 414
International Economic Conditions, 74
International Finance Statistics, 389
International Financial Statistics, 464
International Monetary Market Yearbook, 104
International Reports, 374, 391
Iowa-Nebraska Bank Directory, 75
Italian Credit Structures, 277

Japanese Finance, 280
Journal (Federal Home Loan Bank Board, Washington, DC), 126
Jumbo Rate News, 180

Konjunkturoversigt (Denmark), 256
Kredittmarbedstatistikk (Norway), 300

Leading European Banks, 402
Les banques suisses (Banque nationale suisse), 321
Loan Acceleration Report, 225
Loans Closed and Servicing Volume for the Mortgage Banking Industry, 155
London Currency Report, 415

Magazine of Bank Administration, 91
Main Economic Indicators, 397
Maturity Distribution of International Bank Lending, 344
Memoria (El Salvador), 260
Memoria (Peru), 304
Memoria anual (Bolivia), 240
Memoria: Banco central de Honduras, 267
Memoria del Gerente General del Banco central del Ecuador, 258

Middle East Currency Reports, 416
Middle East Financial Directory, 393
MIDS/Banking and Finance, 465
Midwest Bank Survey (Illinois), 49
Midwest Update (Federal Reserve Bank of Chicago), 65
Mississippi Bank Directory, 26
Mississippi Banker, 26
Mitteilungen (Austria), 232
Modern Gold Coinage, 379
Monetary Review (Denmark), 256
Monetary Statistics (Bank of Jamaica), 278
Monetary Statistics of the United States, 140
Money Market Monitor, 466
Money Market Rates (MRATE), 467
Money Market Services Inc., 468
Money Markets Database, 469
Money Report, 350
Moneywatch, 470
Monthly Bank Clearings, 114
Monthly Bulletin (Bank Indonesia), 272
Monthly Bulletin (Bank of Thailand), 324
Monthly Bulletin (Reserve Bank of New Zealand), 297
Monthly Bulletin of Changes in Bank Activity (Louisiana Department of Commerce), 20
Monthly Digest of Stastics (Hong Kong), 268
Monthly Economic and Financial Statistics (Barbados), 236
Monthly Economic Indicators (Bank of Korea), 314
Monthly Financial Data (Federal Home Loan Bank of Topeka), 62
Monthly Money and Banking Statistics (South African Reserve Bank), 313
Monthly Review (Bank of Jamaica), 278
Monthly Review (Federal Reserve Bank of Kansas City), 68
Monthly Statistical Bulletin (Bangladesh), 235
Monthly Statistical Bulletin (Bank of Guyana), 266

Monthly Statistical Bulletin (Central Bank of Jordan), 282
Monthly Statistical Releases (of U.S. Board of Governors of the Federal Reserve System), 202
Monthly Statistical Report (Federal Home Loan Bank of Des Moines), 56
Monthly Statistical Supplement (Bank Negera. Malaysia), 290
Monthly Statistics of Japan, 279
Monthly Statistics of Korea, 314
Monthly Volume Report: Futures Contract Traded, 141
Moody's Bank and Financial Manual, 153
Morgan Guaranty Survey, 394
Morgan International Data, 395
Mortgage Banking, 156
Mortgage Banking Activity, 157
Mortgage Banking Financial Statements and Operating Ratios, 158
Mortgage Banking Loans Closed and Servicing Volume, 159
Mortgage Banking Survey of Single-Family Loan Operations, 160
Mortgage Index, 471
Mutual Savings Banking, 163

NACHA (National Automated Clearing House Association) Sure Pay Update, 85
NCFA Research Report of Finance Companies, 164
NFIB Quarterly Economic Report for Small Business, 169
National Delinquency Survey, 161
National Economic Trends, 74
National Factbook of Mutual Savings Banking, 186
National Fact Book of Savings Institutions, 166
New Applications: Receipt and Actions Taken, 1
New England Economic Indicators (Federal Reserve Bank of Boston), 64
News (Federal Home Loan Bank Board, Washington, DC), 127
The Nilson Report, 144

Note sur le credit au secteur prive (Burundi), 243
Notes d'information et statistiques (Senegal. Banque centrale des etats de L'Afrique de l'ouest), 346

OECD Economic Outlook, 397
OECD Economic Surveys, 397
Olson BancScore, 172
102 European Banks, 400

Pakistan Banking Directory, 301
Payment Systems in Eleven Developed Countries, 343
Peer Group Report, 121
Perspectives (Federal Home Loan Bank of San Francisco), 60
The Philippine Financial Statistics, 305
Pick World Currency Report, 386, 411
Pick's Currency Yearbook, 386
Plastic Card Float Study, 95
Polk's World Bank Directory, 399
Prime Rates, 472
Private Finance, 231
Prob Database of FOREX Rates, 473
Profile of State Chartered Banking, 108

Quarterly Bulletin (Bank of England), 328
Quarterly Bulletin (Bank of Jamaica), 278
Quarterly Bulletin (Bank of Uganda), 327
Quarterly Bulletin (Central Bank of the Gambia), 263
Quarterly Bulletin (Narodna Bank Jugoslavije), 334
Quarterly Bulletin (Nepal Rastra Bank), 295
Quarterly Bulletin (South African Reserve Bank), 313
Quarterly Economic Bulletin (Bank Negra, Malaysia), 290
Quarterly Economic Bulletin (Bank of Ghana), 264
Quarterly Economic Bulletin (Central Bank of Trinidad and Tobago), 325
Quarterly Financial and Statistical Review (Bank of Zambia), 336
Quarterly Journal (of the U.S. Comptroller of the Currency), 213
Quarterly Report (Federal Home Loan Bank of San Francisco), 60
Quarterly Review (Bank of Mauritius), 292
Quarterly Review (Central Bank of Bahamas), 233
Quarterly Review (Central Bank of Malta), 291
Quarterly Review (Federal Home Loan Bank of Cincinnati), 54
Quarterly Review (Federal Reserve Bank of Minneapolis), 69
Quarterly Review (Federal Reserve Bank of New York), 70
Quarterly Review (National Bank of Hungary), 269
Quarterly Review (Swaziland), 319
Quarterly Review (Swedish National Bank), 320
Quarterly Statistical Bulletin (Bahrain), 234
Quarterly Statistical Releases (of U.S. Board of Governors of the Federal Reserve System), 203
Quarterly Statistical Report (Federal Home Loan Bank of Des Moines), 56
Quarterly Statistical Review (Bank of Sierra Leone), 309
Quarterly Statistical Summary (Central Bank of the Bahamas), 233
Quarterly Statistics (Federal Home Loan Bank of Atlanta), 51
Quarterly Statistics (Nederlandsche Bank), 296
Quarterly Statistics Bulletin (National Bank of Liberia), 286
Quarterly Survey of Agricultural Credit Conditions (Federal Reserve Bank of Dallas), 67

Rapport (Bank of Lebanon), 285
Rapport annuel (Banque de France), 262

Rapport (Morocco), 294
Rapport annuel (Banque de la République du Burundi), 243
Rapport annuel (Banque du Zaire), 335
Rapport annuel (Banque nationale suisse), 321
Rapport annuel (Banques des etats de L'Afrique central), 348
Rapport annuel (Belgium), 237
Rapport d'activité (Banque centrale de Tunisie), 326
Rapport et bilans (Luxembourg), 288
Ratios of Installment Sales Finance and Consumer Finance Corporation, 139
Relatorio Annual, 242
Relazione annuale considerazione finale appendice (Banca d'Italia), 276
Report (European Economic Community), 372
Report (International Savings Banks Institute), 392
Report (Nederlandsche Bank), 296
Report (of Commissioner of Finance, Missouri), 27
Report and Annual Statement of Accounts (Bank of Sierra Leone), 309
Report and Statement of Accounts (Bank of Jamaica), 278
Report of the Bank Commissioner (Arkansas), 4
Report of the Bank Commissioner (Oklahoma), 36
Report of the Board of Directors (Bank of Ghana), 264
Report of the Board of Directors (of Central Bank of Egypt), 259
Report of the Commissioner (of Banking and Financial Institutions, North Dakota), 35
Report of the Commissioner (of the Department of Financial Institutions, Utah), 44
Report of the Governor (Bank of Indonesia), 272
Report of the Monetary Board to the Minister of Finance (Central Bank of Ceylon), 316

Report of the Superintendent of Banks (Oregon), 37
Report on Accounts: Reserve Bank of Malawi, 289
Report on Currency and Finance (Reserve Bank of India), 271
Report on Foreign Countries held by the U.S. Government, 208
Report on Priced Services, 204
Reports of the State Banks, Savings and Loan Associations Credit Unions, Consumer Credit and sale of checks in the State (LA), 20
Reseñā de la actividad economica-financiera (Banco central del Uruguay), 330
Reseña económica financiera y monetaria (Banco central del Paraguay), 303
Resources and Liabilities of Illinois State Banks at the close of Business, 13
Retail Bank Credit Report, 86
A Review of Bank Performance, 179
Review of Federal Home Loan Bank of Atlanta, 4th district, 51
Review of the Economic situation of Mexico, 293
Revista del banco de la república (Colombia), 253
Revista mensual (Banco central de reserva de El Salvador), 260
Revista trimestral (El Salvador), 260

Sales of U.S. Savings Bonds, 219
Saver's Rate News, 181
Savings and Home Financing Source Book, 128
Savings and Loan Fact Book, 222
Savings and Loan Institutions-Deposits by Market in the Chicago SMSAs, 50
The S&L Ratings of all U.S. Savings and Loans, 183
Savings and Loan Summary Statistics (Federal Home Loan Bank of San Francisco), 60
Savings and Loans, 474
The Savings and Loans of Your State, 183
Savings and Mortgage Lending Trends, 223

Title Index   111

Savings Balances and Accounts (Federal Home Loan Bank of San Francisco), 60
Savings Bank Journal, 162
Savings Institutions Sourcebook, 224
Scan, 475
Scheduled Banks Statistics, 235
Securities Industries Trends, 182
Seker (Economic Review) (Bank of Israel), 275
Senior Loan Officer Opinion Survey of Bank Lending Practices, 205
Seventh District Letter (Federal Home Loan Bank of Chicago), 53
Short Form Report (Veribanc), 225
Silver Institute Letter: Information on Silver Industry, 184
Silver Market: An Annual Review, 143
Situation financière (France), 262
South African Statistics, 313
Sparbankerna och föreningsbankerna (Swedish National Bank), 320
Staff Studies (Central Bank of Ceylon), 316
State Average Report, 121
State Chartered Credit Unions: Annual Report, 168
Statement of Foreign Currencies Purchased with Dollars, 209
Statistical Abstract (Bank of England), 328
Statistical Abstract (Bank of Jamaica), 278
Statistical Abstract (Botswana), 241
Statistical Abstract (Central Bank of the Bahamas), 233
Statistical Abstracts (Central Bank of Libya), 287
Statistical Bulletin (Australia), 231
Statistical Bulletin (Botswana), 241
Statistical Bulletin (Central Bank of the Philippines), 305
Statistical Bulletin (National Bank of Liberia), 286
Statistical Digest (Central Bank of Trinidad and Tobago), 325
Statistical Handbook (Bank of Korea), 314
Statistical Summary (Saudi Arabian Monetary Agency), 308
Statistical Yearbook (Central Bank of Jordan), 282
Statistical Yearbook (Narodna Banka Jugoslavije), 334
Statistics Abstract (Cyprus), 255
Statistics of Commercial Banks (Central Bank of Kenya), 284
Statistiques économiques belges, 237
Statistiques mensuelles (France), 262
Statistiske efetrretninger (Denmark), 256
Stistik kenangen (Bank Indonesia), 272
Summary of Actions on Applications Received (Arizona Banking Department), 3
Summary of Savings by Geographic Area, 129
Suplemento estadístico (Bolivia), 240
Supplement on Exchange Rates, 389
Supplement to Banking and Monetary Statistics, 195
Supplemento al Bolletino (Banca d'Italia), 276
Survey of Consumer Finance (Canada), 244
Survey of Finance Companies, 206
Survey of the Check Collection System, 96
Survey of the Electronic Funds Transfer Transaction System, 97
Swiss Capital Markets, 322

Taiwan Financial Statistics Monthly, 252
Telerate-Euromoney World Wide Directory of Foreign Exchange, 369
Tenth District Depository Institutions and Large Commercial Bank Statistics, 68
Texas Banking Red Book, 43
Thrift Institution Activity, 130
Top African Banks, 382
Top 100 Cooperatives: Financial Profile, 191
Treasury Bulletin, 217
The Treasury Information Bulletin, 231

Treasury Report (Euromoney), 370
Treasury Reporting Rates of Exchange, 218
The Trends (Federal Home Loan Bank of Des Moines), 56
Trends in Mutual Fund Activity, 146
Trustcompare, 476
Twelfth District Highlights (Federal Home Loan Bank of Seattle), 61

U.K. Flow of Fund Accounts, 328
Unidex Report, 190
Uniform Bank Performance Report, 121
United States Banks (USBANKS), 477
United States Bonds (USBOND), 478
U.S. Business Outlook: Short Term, 152

Valutastallningen (Finalnd), 261
Veribanc Reports, 225
Verslag (Centrale bank van Suriname), 318
Volume of Futures Trading, 141
Vuosikirja (Yearbook, Bank of Finland), 261

Weekly Bulletin (California Banking Department), 5
Weekly Bulletin (of the U.S. Comptroller of the Currency), 214

Weekly Economic and Foreign Exchange Survey, 479
Weekly Financial Statistics, 244
Weekly Money Report, 113
Weekly Report (Bank Indonesia), 272
Weekly Statistical Releases (of the U.S. Board of Governors of the Federal Reserve System), 207
Western Bank Directory, 77
Western Economic Indicators, 73
Who Owns What in World Banking, 375
Who's Who in Banking in Europe, 405
Who's Who in International Banking, 387
World Banking Monitor, 409
World Currency Charts, 338
World Currency Yearbook, 386
World Debt Tables, 407
World Financial Markets, 396
World Mine Production of Gold, 380
World Monetary Outlook, 401
World Money and Securities Markets, 371
World Outlook, 353
Wrap-up on Latin American Banking and Finance, 342

Y9 (Federal Reserve Board), 480
Yearbook (Swedish National Bank), 320
Yield tables, 178
Yugoslavia in Figures, 334

Subject Index

References are to entry numbers not page numbers.

Accounting practices, 115
Acquisitions, 142, 187, 212, 365, 422
Advertising, 89
Afghanistan, 228
Africa, 346–348, 358, 382. *See also* names of specific countries
African Monetary Union, 347
Agricultural credit, 65, 67, 69, 72, 74
Alabama, 1, 51, 63
Alaska, 2, 61, 73, 77
Algeria, 416
Angola, 229
Antigua, 230
Arizona, 3, 60, 73, 77
Arkansas, 4, 55, 74
Asia, 340, 350, 358, 377, 384. *See also* names of specific countries
ATM. *See* Teller machines
Australia, 231, 377, 413, 418–420
Austria, 232
Automated clearing houses. *See* Clearing houses, Automated
Automatic teller machines. *See* Teller machines

Bahamas, 233
Bahrain, 234, 416
Balance of payments, 421
Bangladesh, 235
Bank crime, 134
Bank failures, 213
Bank holding companies, 88, 119, 183, 225, 423, 437, 480

Bank marketing, 89
Bank performance. *See* Performance measures
Bank regulation, 118, 212, 213, 257, 374
Bank robbery, 81, 134
Banking industry. *See also* Bank holding companies; Chartered banks; Commercial banks; Credit unions; International banking industry; Mutual savings banks; Savings and loan associations; and names of states and countries
 business climate and, 152
 consumer opinions, 190
 databases, 417, 422–424, 432, 437, 440, 442, 447, 465, 479
 directories, 175, 440
 forecasts, 452, 463
 historical data, 192, 192, 195, 201
 news trends, 79
 priced services, 204
 reference books, 100, 101, 153, 226, 345
 reporting practices, 115
 statistical data, 394
Bankruptcies. *See* Bank failures
Barbados, 236
Belgium, 237, 343, 401, 413
Belize, 238
Benin, 239, 346
Biographical data, 387, 405
Bolivia, 240

Bond markets, Domestic. *See*
    Money market instruments
Bonds, Foreign, 339, 341, 350,
    363–368, 373, 396, 397
Bonds, Savings. *See* Savings bonds
Botswana, 241
Brazil, 242
Bullion. *See* Gold; Silver
Burundi, 243
Business conditions, 152, 169, 201,
    350, 432

California, 5, 60, 73, 77
Cameroon, 347
Canada, 106, 244–250, 343, 353,
    413, 427, 429
Capital markets, 102, 360, 368
Central African Empire, 347
Central African Republic, 348
Central America. *See* names of
    specific countries
Chad, 347, 348
Charge-offs, 176
Chartered banks, 107, 108. *See also*
    names of specific states
Check clearings, 114
Check collection, 96
Check fraud, 81
Check routing, 174
Chile, 251
China, 252, 377
Clearing houses, Automated, 85, 97
Coins, 104, 210, 211, 379
Colombia, 253
Colorado, 6, 62, 68
Commercial banks
    business climate and, 152
    databases, 422, 442, 452, 453,
        465, 477
    directories, 149, 151, 398, 399
    FDIC annual report, 118
    financial data, 220, 422, 442,
        453, 465, 477
    forecasts, 452
    newsletter, 145
    performance measures, 177, 179,
        183, 227
    reference books, 403
    state comparisons, 183
Congo, 348
Connecticut, 7, 52, 64, 70
Construction finance. *See* Mortgage
    market

Consumer credit, 84, 87, 137–139,
    164, 442, 452
Cooperatives, 191
Copper, 105
Corporate finance, 107, 145, 361
Costa Rica, 254
Countries. *See* names of specific
    countries and continents
Credit. *See* Consumer credit; Retail
    credit
Credit cards, 80, 82–84, 86, 95, 99,
    144, 171, 173
Credit unions
    databases, 440, 453, 465
    directories, 150, 440
    Illinois, 14
    international data, 410
    state data, 109, 168
    statistical data, 109, 110, 150,
        167, 225, 453, 465
Crime. *See* Bank crime
Currency movements, 208, 209,
    215, 216, 391, 414, 415, 436.
    See also Foreign exchange
    rates
Cyprus, 255

Debt, Foreign, 378, 395, 407, 446
Delaware, 8, 59, 71
Delinquent credit, 82, 83, 161
Denmark, 256, 413
Developing countries, 120, 257,
    407, 446. *See also* names of
    specific countries
District of Columbia, 51, 72
Dominican Republic, 257

Ecuador, 258
EEC. *See* European Economic
    Community
Egypt, 259, 416
El Salvador, 260
Electronic funds transfer. *See*
    Clearing houses, Automated;
    Teller machines
England. *See* United Kingdom
Eurocurrencies
    capital markets, 360, 368
    corporate finance, 361
    currency report, 362
    databases, 456, 457, 473
    debtor organizations, 359
    Euronote and loan data, 364

instruments, 104
international bonds, 363
mergers and acquisitions, 365
monthly data, 396, 411
rates on, 396, 456, 457, 473
trade finance, 366
weekly data, 147, 148
Western European countries, 349
yearbooks, 367, 386
Europe, 343, 349, 350, 372, 376,
  401, 402, 405. *See also* names
  of specific countries
European Economic Community,
  372, 376
Exchange rates. *See* Foreign
  exchange rates
Exchange restrictions. *See* Foreign
  exchange restrictions

Farm loans. *See* Agricultural credit
FDIC. *See* Federal Deposit
  Insurance Corporation
Federal Deposit Insurance
  Corporation, 116–118, 196,
  422, 423, 437
Federal Financial Institutions
  Examination Council, 220
Federal Home Loan Bank
  annual report, 122
  Atlanta district, 51
  Boston district, 52
  Chicago district, 50, 53
  Cincinnati region, 54
  Dallas region, 55
  databases, 437, 474, 475
  Des Moines region, 56
  financial data, 123, 124, 127
  Indianapolis region, 57
  mortgage rates, 125, 126, 128,
    130
  New York region, 58
  Pittsburgh region, 59
  San Francisco region, 60
  savings balances, 129
  Seattle region, 61
  Topeka region, 62
Federal Reserve System
  Atlanta region, 63
  Boston region, 64
  Chicago region, 65
  Cleveland region, 66
  cost analysis, 200
  credits to foreign residents, 196

current statistics, 193, 194, 197,
  202, 203, 207, 394
Dallas region, 67
databases, 423, 437, 443,
  448–451, 477, 480
flow of funds, 198, 199
historical data, 192, 195, 201
Kansas City region, 68
Minneapolis region, 69
money market instruments, 113,
  132, 133, 193–195, 197
New York region, 70
Philadelphia region, 71
priced services, 204
Richmond region, 72
San Francisco region, 73
St. Louis region, 74
Federal Savings and Loan Insurance
  Corporation, 122, 124, 129
FFIEC. *See* Federal Financial
  Institutions Examination
  Council
Finance companies, 206. *See also*
  Consumer finance
Finland, 261
Floats, 95
Florida, 9, 51, 63
Flow of funds, 198, 199, 397, 443,
  454
Foreign banking industry. *See*
  International banking industry
Foreign countries. *See* names of
  specific countries and
  continents
Foreign currencies, 208, 209, 215,
  216
Foreign exchange rates. *See also*
  Currency movements
  analysis of, 371, 432
  Asia and Pacific regions, 384
  databases, 430–435, 438, 439,
    444, 445, 455–457, 463, 464,
    467, 468, 473, 479
  directory of dealers, 369
  forecasts, 353, 362, 430, 432,
    433, 463, 468, 479
  historical data, 338, 351, 434,
    435
  monthly and bimonthly data,
    339, 352, 370, 395, 396, 381,
    385, 411, 414, 415
  newsletter, 374
  quarterly data, 218, 354, 355,

397
time series data, 431, 435
weekly data, 148, 350, 391
yearbooks, 386, 406
Foreign exchange restrictions, 388
Foreign lending, 120, 196, 217, 225, 344, 408, 426
France, 262, 343, 353, 401, 413
FSLIC. *See* Federal Savings and Loan Insurance Corporation
Funds trading system, 458
Futures, 103–105, 141, 369, 370, 411, 436

Gabon, 347, 348
Gambia, 263
Georgia, 10, 51, 63
Germany, 343. *See also* West Germany
Ghana, 264
Gold
  annual data, 386, 388, 400
  coinage, 379
  databases, 456
  historical data, 140
  international data, 354, 386, 388, 412
  prices, 103–105, 411, 412, 414, 456
  production of, 380
  supply and demand, 386, 388
Great Britain. *See* United Kingdom
Guam, 61, 73, 437
Guatemala, 265
Guyana, 266

Hawaii, 11, 61, 73, 77
Home mortgages. *See* Mortgage market
Honduras, 267
Hong Kong, 268, 377, 413
Hungary, 269

Iceland, 270
Idaho, 12, 61, 73, 77
Illinois, 13–15, 49, 50, 53, 65, 74
India, 271
Indiana, 16, 49, 57, 65, 74
Indonesia, 272, 377
Inflation rates, 430
Insolvencies. *See* Bank failures
Installment loans. *See* Consumer credit; Retail credit

Insurance, 81
Interest rates. *See also* Money market instruments
  certificates of deposit, 180
  current data, 147, 148, 395
  databases, 424, 430–433, 438, 439, 442, 444, 452, 457, 463, 464, 466, 468–470, 472
  Eurodollar markets, 349
  Federal Reserve banks, 193, 194, 197
  forecasts, 452, 463, 468, 470
  futures trading, 103
  historical data, 195
  installment credit, 136
  international data, 397
  international monetary market, 104, 413
  medium and small savers, 181
  money market accounts, 78
International banking industry. *See also* names of countries and continents
  annual reports, 351
  balance of payments, 421
  country risk guides, 383, 390
  databases, 438, 441, 444, 445, 461, 464
  directories, 356, 399, 403
  forecasts, 353
  historical data, 351, 434, 435
  international finance, 367, 374, 389
  monetary trends, 386
  money market rates, 467
  newsletter, 409
  performance measures, 357, 374
  rankings, 404
  regulations, 374
  securities markets, 358, 371
  statistical data, 355, 389, 394, 397
  subsidiary and affiliated interests, 375
International bonds. *See* Bonds, Foreign
Iowa, 17, 49, 56, 65, 75
Iraq, 273
Ireland, 274
Israel, 275
Italy, 276, 277, 343, 353, 401, 413
Ivory Coast, 346

Jamaica, 278
Japan, 279–281, 343, 353, 377, 401, 413
Jordan, 282, 416

Kampuchea, 283
Kansas, 18, 62, 68
Kentucky, 19, 49, 54, 66, 74
Kenya, 284
Korea, South, 314, 377
Kuwait, 416

Latin America, 342, 350, 358. *See* names of specific countries
Lebanon, 285
Lending practices, 205
Liberia, 286
Libya, 287, 416
Loan charge-offs, 176
Louisiana, 20, 55, 63, 67
Luxembourg, 288

Maine, 21, 52, 64
Malawi, 289
Malaysia, 290, 377
Malta, 291
Marketing. *See* Bank marketing
Maryland, 22, 51, 72
Massachusetts, 52, 64
Mauritius, 292
Mergers. *See* Acquisitions
Metals. *See* Coins; Copper; Gold; Platinum; Silver
Mexico, 293
Michigan, 23, 49, 57, 65, 69
Middle East, 358, 393, 416. *See also* names of specific countries
Midwest region, 49, 50, 53, 56, 57, 62, 65, 68, 75
Minnesota, 24, 49, 56, 69
Mississippi, 25, 26, 55, 63, 74
Missouri, 27, 49, 56, 68, 74
Money market instruments. *See also* Interest rates
　capital movements between U.S. and foreign countries, 217
　corporate financing, 107
　current data, 395
　Federal Reserve Board data, 113, 132, 133, 193–195, 197
　foreign currencies held by U.S., 208, 215, 216, 219
　futures trading, 103
　historical data, 195
　international data, 104, 135, 395, 396
　national data, 135, 140, 147, 148, 170
Money stock measures. *See* Money market instruments
Montana, 28, 61, 69, 77
Morocco, 294, 416
Mortgage market. *See also* Savings and loan associations
　annual data, 112, 122–124, 128, 166, 221, 224
　databases, 460, 462, 471
　delinquency survey, 161
　directories, 111
　financial and operating data, 154–161
　monthly data, 125–127, 130, 223
　mortgage-backed securities, 178, 460, 462
　prepayment rate yield tables, 178
　secondary mortgage market, 131
Mutual funds, 146
Mutual savings banks, 118, 150, 162, 163, 185, 186, 437

National banks, 212–214
Near East. *See* names of specific countries
Nebraska, 29, 62, 68, 75
Nepal, 295
Netherlands, 296, 343, 401, 413
Nevada, 60, 73, 77
New England region, 52, 64, 76
New Hampshire, 30, 52, 64
New Jersey, 31, 58, 70, 71
New Mexico, 32, 55, 67, 68, 77
New York, 33, 58, 70
New Zealand, 297, 377
Nicaragua, 298
Niger, 346
Nigeria, 299
North Carolina, 34, 51, 72
North Dakota, 35, 56, 69
Northeast region, 52, 58, 59, 64, 70, 71
Northwest region, 61, 73, 77
Norway, 300, 413
NOW accounts, 89

Off-shore banking, 120

Ohio, 49, 54, 66
Oklahoma, 36, 62, 68
Oman, 416
Oregon, 37, 61, 73, 77

Pacific Islands, 340, 384
Pakistan, 301
Paraguay, 303
Payment systems, Foreign, 343
Pennsylvania, 38, 59, 66, 71
Performance measures
  annual reports and 10-K data, 172
  databases, 425
  individual bank profiles, 94
  international data, 357
  operating statistics, 116, 117, 119, 200, 225, 227
  rankings, 79, 183, 227, 404
  ratios for, 93, 94, 98, 119, 121, 179, 188
  savings and loan associations, 188, 227
  state data, 121, 183
Peru, 304
Philippines, 305, 377
Platinum, 411
Prime interest rate. See Interest rates
Puerto Rico, 58, 70, 437

Qatar, 416

Rankings, 79, 183, 227, 404. See also Performance measures
Ratings. See Performance measures; Rankings
Real estate finance. See Mortgage market
Regulations. See Bank regulation
Repossession, 82, 83
Retail credit, 86, 145
Rhode Island, 39, 52, 64
Rwanda, 306

Salaries and wages, 92
Saudi Arabia, 307, 308, 416
Savings banks, 166, 224, 392
Savings bonds, 219, 224, 478
Savings and loan associations. See also Mortgage market
  annual report, 122
  Atlanta district, 51

Boston district, 52
Chicago district, 50, 53
Cincinnati region, 54
Colorado, 6
Dallas region, 55
databases, 437, 440, 452, 453, 465, 474, 475
Des Moines region, 56
directories, 150, 151, 189, 440
directory, 165
financial data, 123, 124, 127
financial indicators, 188
forecasts, 452
Indianapolis region, 57
mortgage rates, 125, 126, 128, 130
New York region, 58
performance measures, 227
Pittsburgh region, 59
ratings, 183
San Francisco region, 60
savings balances, 129
Seattle region, 61
statistical data, 166, 222-225, 227, 225
Topeka region, 62
Securities Exchange Commission, 423
Senegal, 346
Sierra Leone, 309
Silver
  annual data, 103, 105, 400
  coinage, 143
  databases, 456
  industrial uses, 143
  prices, 103, 105, 143, 184, 400, 411, 412, 414, 456
  production of, 184
Singapore, 310, 311, 377, 413
Small business, 169. See also Business conditions
Somalia, 312
South Africa, 313, 413
South America. See names of specific countries
South Carolina, 51, 72
South Dakota, 40, 56, 69
South Korea, 314, 377
South region, 55, 63, 67, 74
Southeast region, 51, 63, 72
Southwest region, 55, 60, 67, 68, 73, 77
Spain, 315, 413

Sri Lanka, 316
State chartered banks. *See* Chartered banks; names of specific states
States. *See* names of specific states
Stock markets, 182, 354, 433
Stock quotations, 170
Sudan, 317
Suriname, 318
Swaziland, 319
Sweden, 320, 343, 413
Switzerland, 321, 322, 343, 401, 413
Syndicated loans, 360
Syria, 416

Tanzania, 323
Teller machines, 89–91, 95, 97
Tennessee, 41, 54, 63, 74
Texas, 42, 43, 55, 67
Thailand, 324, 377
Third world. *See* Developing countries
Tobago, 325
Togo, 346
Trade finance, 366
Treasury instruments. *See* Money market instruments
Trinidad, 325
Trust companies, 106
Trust departments, 476
Tunisia, 326, 416

Uganda, 327

United Arab Emirates, 416
United Kingdom, 328, 329, 343, 353, 401, 403, 413, 428
United States bonds. *See* Savings bonds
Upper Volta, 346
Uruguay, 330
Utah, 44, 61, 73, 77

Venezuela, 331
Vermont, 45, 52, 64
Virgin Islands, 58, 70
Virginia, 46, 51, 72

Washington, 47, 61, 73, 77
Washington, D.C. *See* District of Columbia
West African Monetary Union, 346
West Germany, 332, 353, 401, 413, 459
West region, 60, 61, 73, 77
West Virginia, 59, 66, 72
Western Europe. *See* Europe
Wisconsin, 48, 49, 50, 53, 65, 69
Wyoming, 61, 77

Yemen, 333
Yemens, The, 416
Yugoslavia, 334

Zaire, 335
Zambia, 336
Zimbabwe, 337

M. BALACHANDRAN is Commerce Librarian at the University of Illinois Library at Urbana-Champaign. He is the holder of an MLS from the University of Illinois and a JD from the University of Illinois College of Law. Mr. Balachandran is the author of several reference works in the fields of banking and finance, including *A Guide to Trade and Securities Statistics* and *Regional Statistics: A Guide to Information Sources*.